The Essence of Taijiquan

太極之粹

DAVID GAFFNEY

&

DAVIDINE SIAW-VOON SIM

Copyright © 2012 David Gaffney & Davidine Siaw-Voon Sim

All rights reserved.

ISBN: 1500609234
ISBN-13: 978-1500609238

CONTENTS

page

Foreword	6
Introduction	7

Chapter One
Chenjiagou: The Historical Setting — 17

Chen Bu: Patriarch of the Chen Clan	20
The Birth of Taijiquan	24
Breaking with Tradition	30
The Modern Era	33
The Impact of the Cultural Revolution	38
Chenjiagou Today	45
Village Economy	48
Remembering the Ancestors	50

Chapter Two — 56
Returning to the Source

Philosophical Roots	57
Taiji Theory: Yin and Yang	58
The Eight Trigrams	62
Five Elements	64
The 13 Postures of Taijiquan	69
Daoism and Taijiquan	71
Qi – The Power Source of Taijiquan	73
Understanding the Concept of Qi	74
On Internal Training	80
Yun Qi – Directing Qi	84
Understanding Chansijin	90
Three Sections of the Body	96
The Dantian – Gateway of Yin and Yang	99
Breathing in Taijiquan	103
What Attitude is Required to be Successful?	107
The Three Stages of Progression:	
Opening the Joints	115
Understanding Internal Energy	117
Executing Continuous Movement in One Breath	122

Chapter Three **Taijiquan as a Combat Art**	128
An Internal Martial Art	131
Luihe – The Six Harmonies	133
Form Training – Blueprint for Martial Skills	137
Psychological Attributes	140
Chen Wangting's Boxing Canon	145
Chapter Four **Overlapping Steps**	158
Chen Taiji's Progressive Training Syllabus	159
Zhan Zhuang – Cultivating Stillness	164
How to Practice Zhan Zhuang	169
Chansigong: Silk Reeling Exercises	173
Barehand Forms – The Foundation of Chen Taijiquan Skills	181
Tuishou – To Know One's Opponent	192
Supplementary Drills for Tuishou	204
Classical Weapons Training	206
Jian (Sword)	207
Dao (Broadsword)	210
Qiang (Spear)	213
Chunqiu Dadao (Spring & Autumn Broadsword)	216
Chapter Five **Insights**	220
Chen Xiaowang: Preserving a Legacy	221
Chen Xiaoxing: Understanding the Taolu	231
Zhu Tiancai on Chen Taijiquan's Fajin	245
Chen Ziqiang: The Four Essential Elements of Martial Skill	250
Wang Haijun on the Bafa of Taijiquan	259
Tian Jingmiao – A Woman's Perspective	267
Chen Zhenglei - Taijiquan: Ancient Art or New Age Fad?	276

David Gaffney & Davidine Siaw-Voon Sim

The Essence of Taijiquan 太極之粹

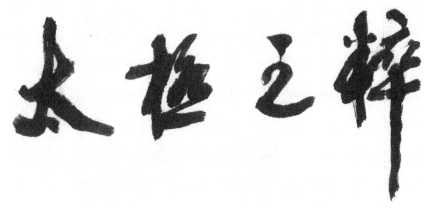

"The Essence of Taijiquan" – Calligraphy by Chen Xiaowang

Foreword

David Gaffney and Davidine Siaw-Voon Sim have studied Taijiquan seriously with me for many years now. They have been diligent in their practice and achieved good results. Their previous book Chen Style Taijiquan: The Source of Taiji Boxing has consistently had good reviews. As I travel the world teaching my family's art, I have seen how welcome and well received it has been. I have every confidence that this new work will be of equal standard and would recommend it to all those with a love of Chen Taijiquan without any reservations.

Chen Xiaowang
19th Generation Gatekeeper of Chen Family Taijiquan

INTRODUCTION

"Man is made of flesh and spirit both, and it should be the philosopher's business to see that the mind and body live harmoniously together, that there be a reconciliation between the two."

(Lin Yutang, 1951)

Taijiquan 太极拳 is no ordinary martial art. More than the sum of its parts Taijiquan is: a valuable method for enhancing health; a means of cultivating calmness and balance; an engaging leisure pursuit; and a tried and tested method of self-defence. At its highest level, it is a complete life enriching principle. Studying Taiji, a person can come to appreciate important aspects of one of the world's most ancient culture, especially the philosophy of change – the *yin-yang* study contained in the *yijing*.

When Taijiquan was created four centuries ago it was no different from other types of martial arts, its primary intention being to maximise the combat ability of its followers. However, since the invention of firearms and towards the end of the Qing Dynasty martial arts in China have undergone a slow transformation until today when the majority of people practice primarily for health or performance. Today many traditional martial arts are a pale shadow of their former selves.

This is particularly true in the case of Taijiquan, which has become a popular exercise for older people over the last few decades. According to statistics quoted in China's *Wulin* 武林 (Martial World) magazine upwards of eighty percent of Taiji practitioners are middle-aged or elderly. While no exact figures are available it seems obvious that the same holds true in the West. This by itself is not a bad thing as long as practitioners can differentiate between Taijiquan and Taiji exercise. More pernicious in recent decades has been the emergence of a generation of zealous Taiji practitioners who turn their noses up at the traditional martial arts philosophy of Taijiquan. Armed with the most superficial understanding of Taijiquan they promote the art as a kind of pseudo-spiritual new age practice. Little wonder that practitioners of other martial arts question whether Taijiquan is usable or even if it is a martial art at all.

However, the real thing still exists. Chenjiagou 陈家沟, situated deep within the countryside of Henan 河南 province, has carried on China's rural martial tradition. It was here that the art of Taijiquan was created in the late seventeenth century and despite social and political upheaval, changing lifestyles and the coming of the modern era it continues to hold to the time-honoured method of developing gongfu skills. These skills, which have been refined over the centuries by generations of battle-hardened fighters, can be learned neither quickly nor easily. However, there is no secret skill transmitted only to a chosen few disciples. Taijiquan is at heart a practical physical discipline.

Chen Family Taijiquan 陈氏太极拳, the original style from which all other styles have evolved from, has its own unique approach and can be pigeonholed by neither hardness nor softness. Instead it aims to alternate between the two poles until a middle path is accomplished. At this point it can be said that the *yin-yang* 阴阳 principle has been grasped. For the outsider looking in, or for the beginning student facing the barriers of language and culture, the requirements of the art can seem impossibly demanding. Yet Taijiquan has been practiced successfully by generations of people in the simple village where it was created nearly four centuries ago. Why then does the process seem so complicated?

Chen Xiaowang 陈小旺, the current Gatekeeper 掌门人 of Chen Taijiquan, likens it to the educational process where each stage of learning logically builds upon the preceding one: *"Learning Taijiquan and learning in school are the same. From primary school to university, one accumulates more and more knowledge. If one is without the foundation of a primary and secondary school education, it will be impossible to assimilate the syllabus of a university education. Similarly, learning Taijiquan must be done in the correct order, advancing gradually, level by level. If one goes against this order, like a primary school goer trying to understand the lessons of a university, it will be like 'pulling up a shoot to hasten growth* 拔苗助长*'. The end result will be 'speeding but failing to arrive* 欲速则不达*'"* (Chen Xiaowang - Zhonghua Wushu magazine 中华武术杂志).

In a similar vein, Chen Style Taijiquan exponent Zhu Tiancai朱天才 suggested that the processes of learning Taijiquan and learning to write the Chinese characters shared the same principles. *"At the beginning you just learn the horizontal stroke, the upright stroke, the tick and the tail. You repeatedly and exactly write these strokes – that is the basic training. Once the basics are established and you become proficient, then you can go on to practice the writing style with flourish. At the same time you still adhere to the rules of writing because you cannot move away from the rule. All the strokes and lines should still follow the same sequence. Learning Taijiquan should follow the same principle as you progress level-by-level, improving within the rules and principles. If you go against this rule then you will not arrive – that is you won't reach the destination you are hoping for because you are not following the correct route".*

Many aspects of Taijiquan are far from obvious even when a highly skilled teacher demonstrates. A teacher's knowledge and explanation is an essential part of the learning process. But no matter how skilled the teacher is it ultimately counts for nothing unless it is accompanied by a student's practice and understanding. While the teacher demonstrates, the student must take responsibility for his or her own learning. Each individual has his/her own unique physical make up and, no matter how much they may want to, cannot (and indeed must not) become an exact reproduction of their teacher. When listing the attributes necessary for an individual to realise a high level of skill, the Chinese traditionally listed the importance of *wuxing*悟性, or a person's innate ability to grasp facts, alongside having a good teacher and possessing good physical ability. What is completely within a practitioner's own sphere of influence is how diligently they practice. There are no secrets. Generations of Chen Taijiquan boxers have sought to *"lian gong ti hui* 练功体会*"* or to attain "realisation through training the body". If there were a secret it would be persistent training allied to confidence and belief in the method handed down.

There needs to be patience and a degree of faith in the training method. It is easy to see how dedicated practitioners, particularly in the West, can inadvertently go down the wrong path. Students learning within Chenjiagou have the significant advantage of learning within an environment with visible role models at each stage of attainment. The steps are quite clear. Today, we live in a global village, where everyone has access to information and quality instruction. Many Western practitioners' only experience is through seminars with the highest-level teachers. This is a wonderful opportunity not open to many Chinese students, but one must not forget that the grandmasters represent the endpoint in a highly structured training process.

The Essence of Taijiquan 太极之粹 seeks to address the fundamental nature of the system in a practical manner, and in the process looks to refute some of the popular stereotypes that have come to be associated with Taijiquan. Chapter One delves into the history of the Chen Village (Chenjiagou) and the dramatic social, political and environmental factors that have shaped the birthplace of Taijiquan. From the establishment of the village in an area devastated by the homicidal brutality of the first Ming Emperor; to the creation of Taijiquan by ninth generation descendant Chen Wangting, exiled to the village after the collapse of the same dynasty some three centuries later; to the turmoil of the Mao-inspired Cultural Revolution and the persecution of traditional family arts such as Taijiquan; finally to the new economic prosperity and "opening" of China and with it the worldwide spread of Taijiquan.

Chapter Two examines the nature of Taijiquan as a combat art. As well as considering the physical and psychological nature of the system, it examines Chen Wangting's *Boxing Canon* 拳经, the most ancient text surviving in Chenjiagou. In this concise manuscript the essential character of Chen style Taijiquan is outlined. While interpreting the early Chinese text is difficult it offers unique insights into the art as it was practiced in the past. The chapter also seeks to explain why Taijiquan is described as an "internal" martial art and to elucidate the concept of *Lui He* 六合 or the "Six Harmonies" which must be understood if the body is to operate as an integrated system rather than as a collection of isolated body parts.

Finally considered is the traditional emphasis upon form training as a blueprint for martial skills. Without a thorough understanding of the reasoning behind the use of form training as the fundamental skill-building method of Taijiquan, form can easily degenerate into mere formalism. Today many people mistakenly think that Taijiquan's form training is the process of training gongfu, not realising that the gongfu training and the health benefits arising from Taijiquan practice are two separate entities. Perhaps this is why many sincere practitioners lament their lack of combat skill after decades of Taiji training. The process of training gongfu requires Taijiquan practitioners to understand the martial art of Taijiquan and the health building elements of Taijiquan and the difference between the two.

By and large the literary tradition of Taijiquan has been presented as a litany of the esoteric in modern times. Contrast this with the practical realities of a martial system created by a battle-hardened veteran and jealously guarded by generations of Chen clan members, many of who were employed as bodyguards for rich merchant caravans. As late as the twentieth century the art was still being used in deadly earnest. At a time when the West was consumed by the industrial scale slaughter of "modern" warfare during the First World War, in China's lawless interior Chen Fake 陈发科 was still using Taijiquan and traditional weaponry to defend the settlement of Wenxian from roving gangs of bandits.

It would seem logical then that the training advice left behind was intended to offer practical guidance for those reading it. Using the writings of Chen Zhaopi 陈照丕, the eighteenth generation great master of Chen Family Taijiquan, as a template, Chapter Three examines a number of the philosophical concepts that underpin Taijiquan to make sense of them from a modern standpoint. Included is: an examination of Yin-Yang theory, the Five Elements and how Chen Zhaopi linked them with actual movements within the form; the *Bagua* 八卦 or Eight Trigrams and their association with the eight intrinsic energies of Taijiquan; there is an analysis of *Qi* 气, the "power source of Taijiquan". To share a common understanding of the complex concept of Qi with past generations of practitioners this "vital energy" is examined within its cultural context. While there are many difficulties in crossing the barriers of language, history and culture, Chen Zhaopi's classification of Qi offers a window through which today's Taijiquan exponents can experience Qi on a tangible level. He organised *Qi* into five clear or positive *Qi* that are to be cultivated by the Taijiquan practitioners, and five stagnant or negative *Qi* to be eliminated. While couched in language that may appear esoteric, his classification is eminently practical with clear physical markers to be looked for at different stages of an individual's development. After establishing how to recognise the presence of Qi within the body Chen Zhaopi discusses the meaning of *Yun Qi* 运气 or circulating and moving Qi.

Generations of Chen Style Taijiquan teachers have suggested that there are a series of distinct stages a practitioner must go through on the road to mastery. Developing skill in the traditional way is a long-term undertaking requiring patience and perseverance. As Chen Xin 陈鑫 of the sixteenth generation and author of the first Chen Taijiquan book, put it: *"practicing Taiji requires progressive advancement. You cannot skip the stages of progression"*. Chen Changxin 陈长兴, the fourteenth generation gatekeeper of Chen Taijiquan summarised these stages in the expression: *"from familiarity with postures, to understanding jin 劲 and from understanding jin to attain enlightenment"*. Enlightenment or *"shen ming 神明"* refers to a realisation of the true nature of Taijiquan. At this point, the practitioner's external shape and internal energy are said to coordinate perfectly. Chen Zhaopi wrote that these stages progress as your movements go *"from big circles to middle circles from middle circles to small circles, and from small circles to indiscernable circles. To skip a stage is not feasible. One cannot bypass the big and medium circles and go straight into the small and indiscernable circles"*.

Chapter Three also outlines Chen Zhaopi's "Three stages of Achievement" which provide Taijiquan practitioners with a clear progressive path to follow from the novice stages through to mastery. Stages include opening the joints and training the external energy; understanding internal energy where he lists thirteen characters whose study forms the basis of Taiji's *neijin* 内劲 or internal energy; and the final stage where all techniques are merged within the body ready to be brought out at will, which he called *"one breath coordinating all movements* 一气呵成", using sixteen characters broken down into four character sayings to illustrate the third level of gongfu.

Chapter Four looks at Chen Family Taijiquan's progressive training syllabus. *Zhan Zhuang* 站桩 (Standing Pole) integrates the elements of posture, relaxation and breathing. It provides a means of developing improved alignment and balance ; leg and waist strength ; deeper respiration ; precise body awareness ; and a calm mind. Barehand forms provide the foundation of Chen Taijiquan skills. First learn the core movement principles and working to achieve standardised movement. Students are trained to move in ways that at times seem incredibly complex and even unnatural. With persistence any deficiencies in terms of positioning and movement are gradually overcome, and the body begins to respond to one's mental commands, as it should.

Each of the traditional styles of Taijiquan possesses their own unique postural framework and mode of expression. For this reason, it is important to make a choice and then persevere with it. As far as Chen Taijiquan is concerned, debates on the relative merits of Old or New Frame Taijiquan are of little consequence. Of paramount importance is choosing a good teacher to learn from. The subtleties of Taijiquan cannot be learned by buying a book and studying the postures. Many Taijiquan books are filled with pages of pictures depicting the movements from the various forms. However, these fixed postures cannot demonstrate the complexities of the Taijiquan forms. The true image and complexity of Taijiquan is hidden deeply within the transition movement between two fixed postures. During these transition movements, there are a multitude of corresponding internal changes within the practitioner's body that can never be captured in a still photograph. The *quan li* 拳理 (philosophy) and *quan fa* 拳法 (method) are entirely contained within this transition. To transmit the subtle nature of these changes requires the student to have access to verbal instruction and physical demonstration of a good and knowledgeable teacher.

In time one learns to concentrate, to physically settle the body and to relax those muscles that are unnecessary for performing a movement. As one's level of skill increases, the next goal is to search for a deeper awareness of the internal distribution of energy. Chen Taijiquan's spiral and arc movement is based on accurate co-ordination of movements, proper alignment of the whole body internally and externally, and is a practice skill to enable the body's internal energy to be distributed throughout the body (channels and meridians that influence the whole body). Little by little the critical, logical part of the mind is quieted. Since the time of the ancient Greeks, Western culture has been characterised by independence, verbal contention and debate. Individuals analyse the world rationally from the perspective of discreet objects and their unique properties. *"Our Western way of viewing the world lends itself to separating out components of a whole in order to examine them more closely, sometimes forgetting that it is the working of the whole that is important"* (Kauz, 1989). The correctness of the form is validated through push hands practice that also heightens one's combat skills.

Chapter Five is entitled "Insights". In an extensive series of interviews it endeavours to get to the heart of Chen Family Taijiquan through the perspectives of a number of Taijiquan exponents of different generations and ages. They relate their own understanding and experience of what the art entails. This offers a stark dichotomy between the mental and physical discipline of an ancient martial tradition and the modern perception held by the majority of players of the great art as being a pleasant form of exercise and recreation.

Chen Xiaowang陈小旺 reflects on his life journey, relating some of the influences that led to him to become one of the most travelled and famous Chinese martial artists in the world today – from the early training years where he wanted simply to live up to his family legacy to his decision to take Taijiquan overseas; Chen Xiaoxing陈小星, the Principal of the Chenjiagou Taijiquan School in its birthplace, describes the various handforms in the Chen Taijiquan curriculum and their unique features. He also tells of his own Taijiquan path and his thoughts on the state of Taijiquan today; His eldest son Chen Ziqiang陈之强, the head coach of the village school, compares traditional and modern approaches to Taijiquan training and outlines what he believes are the four essential elements of martial skill; In an interview first broadcast by BBC Radio's Eastern Horizon programme, nineteenth generation inheritor Chen Zhenglei 陈正雷 speaks of the approach needed to successfully take Taijiquan forward into the twenty-first century; In a slightly different vein Tian Jingmiao 田京苗, a member of the Beijing Chen Style Taijiquan Research Centre, describes what it was like being the only female disciple to learn from Lei Muni 雷慕尼, a famous disciple of Chen Fake 陈发科, the renowned seventeenth generation standard bearer of the Chen Family. She also offers some words of advice on the correct approach needed to make a success of one's Taijiquan practice as well as addressing some of the issues facing women studying Chen style Taijiquan; Wang Haijun 王海军 a senior disciple of Chen Zhenglei and a China National Gold Medalist in Taijiquan offers an analysis of Taijiquan's *Bafa* 八法 i.e. the eight methods of training the body's intrinsic energies (*jin*) that together provide the foundation of all the skills and techniques of Taijiquan; Finally Zhu Tiancai 朱天才 one of the "Four Buddha's Warriors" of Chenjiagou explains the process of developing effective *fajin* 发劲 (explosively emitting power) skills.

Throughout this closing chapter the thoughts of the different teachers lead one to feel a deep sense of history. Even more important than recorded history is that which has not been recorded, but passes down as legends from mouth to mouth, father to son, teacher to student. The most

important knowledge of mankind has at times been handed down in this way. For today's western exponents this sense of history and of linage points the way to truly "entering the door" of real Taijiquan practice. For the art to maintain its integrity western instructors of this ancient eastern discipline and philosophy must become a bridge between the two cultures reconciling their western socialisation with their eastern art. Teaching with the knowledge that they are one of a long chain of students and teachers – neither the first, nor the last.

The Essence of Taijiquan 太極之粹

Chenjiagou Taijiquan Museum

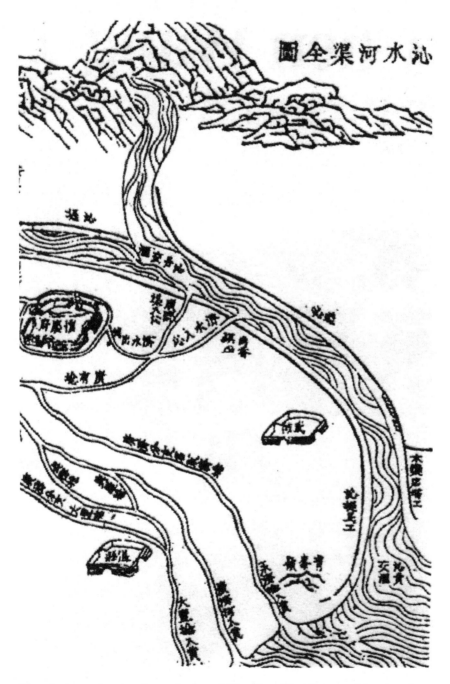

Historical map showing the settlement of Qing Feng Ling (bottom right corner), which later became known as **Chenjiagou**.

CHAPTER ONE

CHENJIAGOU: THE HISTORICAL SETTING

Located in the centre of Henan河南 province in Central China, Chenjiagou陈家沟 is not an obvious tourist destination. It is an unremarkable rural village like many others in China. Yet it draws thousands of visitors throughout the year, as this village is acknowledged to be the birthplace of Taijiquan.

Often referred to simply as the "Taiji Village", Chenjiagou is surrounded by the four large cities of Xinxiang新乡 on the east, Zhengzhou郑州 on the south, Luoyang洛阳 on the west and Jiaozuo焦作 on the north. It is acknowledged as one of the most significant martial arts locations in China, alongside the Shaolin Temple少林寺 and the Wudang mountains武当山. Taijiquan, one of the major branches of Chinese Martial Arts, has been practiced here for generations and continues to this day. A brief examination of the recent history of Chenjiagou shows how difficult it has been for the village to preserve its legacy. A combination of political, social and environmental factors has conspired to challenge the very survival of Taijiquan in its birthplace.

The Historical Patriarch of the Chen Clan

The Chen clan of Chenjiagou can trace its ancestry back to Chen Bu, the historical patriarch. Chen Bu 陈卜 founded the village during the turbulent years when the Yuan Dynasty 元朝 (1271-1368) was coming to an end and the formation of the Ming Dynasty 明朝 (1368-1644). It was a time of war and devastation; law and order were non-existent and the population lived in poverty and fear. The warrior *Zhu Yuanzhang* 朱元璋 eventually emerged victorious and took control of China and founded the Ming dynasty. The fate of Chen Bu was determined during this time.

Zhu Yuanzhang's men carried out a raid to the Huaiqing 怀庆 prefecture (today's Qinyang city 沁阳市, which in those days governed eight counties, including *Wen* County 温县 where Chenjiagou is located), where they encountered fierce resistance from the Yuan general *Tie Muer* 铁木耳 and sustained huge casualties. However, a single prefecture could not hold off the sustained attack of the vast army of Zhu Yuanzhang and it was finally defeated because of the lack of supplies and reinforcements, and the few remaining Yuan soldiers dispersed. The consequences for the region were catastrophic. "After Zhu Yuanzhang ascended the throne, he turned his anger on the population of *Huaiqing* Prefecture, accusing them of helping the resistance against the imperial soldiers. He sent his solders to carry out the three "cleansings" of Huaiqing 三洗怀庆 by slaughtering the whole population. It is said that after the Ming soldiers finished pillaging a place, they often left money, food, clothes, etc. at the crossroad in the centre of a village. If these items were picked up, a new search would ensue. Although people went into hiding with their families, eight to nine out of ten did not manage to escape the massacre. After the three "cleansings" of the prefecture and its eight counties, an area of several thousand square kilometres were littered with blood and bodies. Almost no crops could be seen and not a single rooster could be heard in the thousand villages". (Chen Xiaowang, 2004)

Historical records of the period tell of the implementation of a policy of mass migration and wasteland reclamation. A migration office was

The Scholar Tree in Shanxi province from which the Chen family ancestors trace their roots.

established in Shanxi 山西 Province, and local inhabitants were compelled to relocate to the now sparsely populated areas devastated by the war (one of which was Huaiqing Prefecture). Among those forced to move was Chen Bu, who is known to have "originated from Dongtuhe village 东土河村, Zezhou 泽州 (today's Jincheng 晋城), Shanxi. In the first year of *Hongwu 洪武 (1368), Chen Bu fled with his family from famine to

Chen family temple mural - Chen Bu setting out from beneath a scholar tree in Shanxi.

Hongdong洪洞. In the fifth year of Hongwu he was amongst the people who were forced to move to Henan's Huaiqing Prefecture". Since the traditional starting point for all migrations was beneath a scholar tree (h*uaishu*槐树), the saying persists today that the Chen family ancestors came from *Shanxi Big Scholar Tree*祖先来之大槐树.

Upon arrival at the designated region, Chen Bu settled in the south-eastern section, with the Yellow River to the south, Taihang Mountains in the north, and a wide fertile flood plain. A village was gradually established which was named *Chen Bu Zhuang*陈卜庄 (Chen Bu's village). The village bears his name to this day though it is now part of Wen County instead of Qinyang. The village, however, was situated on low-lying ground and was prone to flooding. Chen Bu therefore moved to a location five kilometres to the east to *Qing Feng Ling* 清风岭 (Green Wind Ridge). The village was called Chang Yang Village 常阳村. Chen Bu settled there and became famous for leading an attack to destroy a nearby bandit stronghold that had been terrorising the village. As his reputation grew he established a martial arts school in order to train the villagers to defend themselves.

Despite his many heroic exploits the eventual way the village acquired its name is somewhat prosaic. "Areas on both sides of the Yellow River were frequently flooded. Many failed attempts were made to deepen the river. Parallel drainage ditches, therefore, were created to help deal with floodwaters. These came to be associated with families. Chen Bu's family name gave Chang Yang Village its modern name of *Chenjiagou*陈家沟, meaning "Chen Family Ditch". The name *gou*沟, which means drainage ditch, was attached to "Chen family" *(Chen Jia*陈家*)*" (Gaffney and Sim, 2002).

The "Chen family ditch" today

The Birth of Taijiquan

While the art of Taijiquan was yet to make an appearance the martial tradition of the Chen clan continued. The Chen family was famous for several generations for their Cannon Fist (*Paocui*炮捶) Boxing and was known as the "Paocui Chen Family" *(炮捶陈家)"* (Gaffney and Sim, 2002).

Detailed historical records of people, events and martial arts in Chenjiagou started from the time of Chen Wangting陈王庭 (1600-1680), the person who created Taijiquan. According to the *Annals of Huaiqing Prefecture*怀庆志 *and Wen County Annals*温县志, Chen Wangting was a military officer and served as Commander in the Garrison Force of Wen County in 1641, just before the fall of the Ming dynasty. The *Genealogy of Chen Families*陈氏家谱 stated that at the end of the Ming dynasty Chen Wangting was already famous for his martial skills, "*having once defeated more than 1000 bandits and was a born warrior, as can be proven by the sword he used in combat.*" (Gaffney and Sim, 2002).

Some three centuries earlier the Emperor Hongwu had established a powerful military machine with a million-man standing army. This was divided into basic garrison units or *wei*卫 of roughly five thousand men which were further subdivided into smaller companies known as *suo* 所. For major campaigns, soldiers were assembled from *wei* and *suo* from the four corners of the country under the instruction of commanders from the capital. However, by Chen Wangting's time, in the final years of the Ming dynasty, the *wei-suo* 卫所system had become a bureaucratic nightmare.

According to Charles Hucker (1975) "…the *wei-suo* standing army declined in strength and fighting ability. It was supplemented by local militiamen, then by conscripts from the general population, and finally in the last Ming century by recruited mercenaries in awesome numbers. In the last Ming

Chen Wangting statue at the Chen Family Temple in Chenjiagou

decades the military rolls swelled to a reported total of four million men. But they were poorly equipped, ill trained, and irregularly fed and clothed; only a small fraction of the total can have been effective soldiers".

Chen Wangting was fiercely loyal to the Ming dynasty and its fall put paid to any ambitions of advancement he held. Consequently he retired to Chenjiagou where he lived out the rest of his days. It is not hard to imagine the frustration that this warrior, pensioned off at the peak of his powers, must have felt. It was during this period that he began to compile a unique form of martial art that combined various disciplines and assimilated the essence of many martial skills in existence at the time.

In developing his new art Chen Wangting appears to have been heavily influenced by the famous general and outstanding military strategist Qi Jiguang戚继光 (1528-1587). Chen Xiaowang (2004) wrote that: "Chen Wangting and Qi Jiguang were not of the same dynasty, but Chen admired Qi's patriotism and the way he had absorbed the best of the various martial schools. He was especially influenced by Qi's arrangement of the different martial systems. Society was in turmoil during the period of Chen Wangting's middle age and the country was being invaded by foreigners. Unable to do his duty for the country and unable to fulfil his ambitions, Chen Wangting retired to the village with his constant companion "*Huangting Jing*黄庭内外景经" (*The Yellow Chamber's Internal and External Canon*) with the intention of organising the different martial arts systems of his time. In this way Chen Wangting, following Qi Jiguang, is celebrated for the research and collation of folk martial arts. This was the base from where he later created Taijiquan".

Between 1559 and 1561, General Qi compiled *Ji Qiao Xin Shu* 紀效新书 (New Book of Effective Techniques), his classic text on strategy and martial arts. The comprehensive manual comprised of fourteen chapters, four of which are dedicated to the practice of *wushu*武术. The most widely quoted chapter is the *"Quan Jing*拳经" (Canon of Boxing), which depicts an

The writings of the famous general and outstanding military strategist Qi Jiguang heavily influenced Chen Wangting in his creation of Taijiquan.

effective and powerful repertoire assimilating the arts of sixteen different martial systems of the time. From this Qi developed a boxing routine that comprised of thirty-two forms selected from what he considered to be the foremost styles of the day.

Qi stressed the necessity of rigorous physical fitness training and effective hand-to-hand tactics and not accepting the superiority of brute strength alone as the determining factor in battle. He called for the sophisticated use of brain over brawn to give the greatest chance of success in hand-to-hand combat. This is particularly evident in one chapter in his manual where Yu Dayou's 俞大猷 (1503-1580) *Sword Classic*剑经 was included in its entirety. One of Yu's verses advises combatants to, "*Use hard force prior to the opponent's release of force. While the opponent is busy, I calmly wait; I observe his rhythm and let him struggle*". In an essay entitled *General Qi Jiguang's Approach to Martial Arts Training*, Stanley Henning (1995) wrote, "*The key to Yu's tactics is, "Take advantage of the point where his old force has passed and before his new force is released*". He concluded that the theories espoused in military martial arts texts from the Ming period are similar to those that would later appear in the Taijiquan classics.

General Qi was most famous for successfully defending China against rampaging pirates from Japan. He also successfully defeated the Mongolian invaders from the north. His tactics involved feigning weakness and retreating before the enemy. After leading them far inland and lulling them into a false sense of superiority, Qi's forces overwhelmed the invaders in a sudden and decisive counterattack (Millinger and Fang, 1976). This was to be adopted by Chen Wangting to become Taijiquan's central tenet of *"not meeting strength with strength"* and *"leading an opponent into emptiness"*.

Qi's works presented a compellingly practical application of the best in Chinese military practice. They also clearly show that, even in his day, the martial arts practiced within the small rural communities as part of militia training had gradually become diluted until it owed as much to recreation and self-expression as it did to actual combat efficacy. Like Chen Wangting later, Qi placed great emphasis on martial effectiveness deriding the use of "flowery" martial arts as undisciplined and inappropriate for military use in combat. The fact that a movement might be spectacular to look at cut little ice with Qi if it was of no practical value. As he unambiguously put it, *"…in training troops, the pretty is not practical and the practical is not pretty…"* (Henning, 1995).

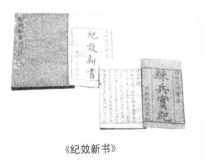

《纪效新书》

General Qi Jiguang's classic text on strategy and martial arts – Ji Qiao Xin Shu (New Book of Effective Techniques)

Chen, however, did more than simply incorporate the essential theories of Qi Jiguang. His new system was highly innovative adding *"the novel concepts of hiding firmness in softness and using different movements to overcome the unpredictable and changing moves of the opponent, thereby raising external fighting skills to a higher level. Power is generated from within, with the use of "internal energy to become outward strength".* This theory is embodied in Chen's "Song of the Canon of Boxing拳经总歌": *"Actions are varied and executed in a way that is completely unpredictable to the opponent, and I rely on twining movements and numerous hand-touching actions".* "Hand-touching" denotes the close contact of the arms to develop sensitivity to react quickly--*"nobody knows me, while I alone know everybody"*".

Excerpt from Qi Jiguang's Canon of Boxing

Breaking With Tradition

"If you meet multiple opponents who surround you, appear strong like a living dragon or tiger, attack one opponent, with the power of a large cannon booming straight".

- Chen Changxing

Chen Changxing

Up until the time of Chen Changxing陈长兴 (1771-1853), the fourteenth generation of the Chen Clan, Taijiquan was a closely guarded secret within the Chen family. Chen Changxing had a formidable reputation as a *biaoshi*镖师 (martial escort), commissioned to protect merchant caravans during their passage through neighbouring bandit lands, particularly the Shandong Province, during a period of considerable lawlessness and social unrest. And it was he who first broke with family tradition and rearranged the martial art created by Chen Wanting.

The safe transportation of goods at that time was extremely difficult and relied entirely on men and horse drawn transport. Bandits and robbers often ambushed the goods along the way, making it necessary for merchants to hire *biaoshi* to protect their merchandise in order to ensure safe passage. Chinese classical literature such as *The Water Margin* 水虎专 depicts heroic tales of the individuals who carried out these roles. Since the Tang and Song dynasties the profession of *biaoshi* 镖师 (master who protects the goods) or *baobiao* 保镖 (guardian of the goods) was invariably undertaken by highly skilled martial artists. Famous *biaoshi* included *Xingyiquan's* Dai Wenxiong 戴文熊 who acted as an escort in the Beijing area in the early nineteenth century, *Mizongquan* 迷踪拳 boxer Huo Yuanjia 霍元甲, portrayed by Jet Li in the film Fearless and Wang Xianzhai 王芗斋, the creator of *Dachenquan* 大成拳 (Yu, 2003).

Guarding a merchant caravan – scene from the Chen Family Temple

From the beginning of the Qing dynasty the profession of *biaoshi* was formalised. Companies were established whose sole concern was to escort traders and their valuables. Whether the company was successful or not depended entirely upon the safe delivery of goods and personnel to their destination. Therefore the primary concern of each of these companies was to protect their reputation. If an escort company was robbed three times it was shut down. Consequently those employed as escorts were usually highly skilled as well as with a good reputation (Yu, 2003).

Historian Charles O. Hucker's (1975) vivid description of the period suggests that Chen Changxing's reputation must have been hard earned. Chen Changxing lived during the time of the *Nian* Rebellion捻军起义, whose roots can be traced back to the last decade of the eighteenth century, among itinerant groups of bandits operating in the border-region area that comprised southwest Shandong, northwest Jiangsu, east-central Henan, and northern Anhui. Hucker described the rebels as: *"a rootless and volatile group capable of swinging into action with a raiding party at any time… The settled local communities tried to guarantee some security by establishing small protective militias, walled villages and crop-watching associations, but the Nian nevertheless launched raids to seize crops from nearby villages, to rob transport vehicles of government salt merchants, or to kidnap wealthy landlords for ransom".*

The original art of Chen Wangting comprised of five boxing routines. For practical reasons, Chen Changxing synthesized them into what is known today as the *Laojia Yilu* 老架一路 (Old Frame First Routine) and *Laojia Erlu* 老架二路 (Second Routine), also known as the *Paocui* 炮捶 or Cannon Fist Form. These forms make up the foundation forms from which subsequent generations of Chen Village practitioners have developed their capabilities until the present day. The change made to the original forms represents the biggest change of all in the evolution of Chen Taijiquan. He further developed Taijiquan theory and his surviving writings *"Ten important Discourse on Taijiquan*太极拳十大要论*", "Important Words on Taijiquan Applications*太极拳用武要言*",* and *"A Chapter on Taijiquan Combat*太极拳战斗篇*"* greatly benefited future generations of practitioners enriching the theoretical discourse of Taijiquan.

Chen Changxing's second momentous break with tradition was to teach Taijiquan to Yang Luchan 杨露禅 (1799-1871) – the first time the family system had been transmitted to anyone outside the Chen clan. Today this may not seem a big deal, but at that time the significance of the clan cannot be over-emphasised. In fact the secrecy of the rural family clans is one important reason why many family martial systems were able to develop their own unique characteristics and flavour. A vital condition for the development of the many local fighting systems was the patriarchal family system. The primary importance traditionally placed in the family, it's setting itself strictly apart from other clans and its autonomous way of life preserved the distinctive family combat systems over generations. Outsiders were strictly excluded from learning the clan secrets. By breaking this taboo, Chen Changxing paved the way for the development of the widely practiced Yang style Taijiquan and thereon to other Taiji styles.

Today when most people practice martial arts for sport, health and recreation it is easy to lose sight of the life and death seriousness of martial

Entrance to the courtyard where Chen Changxing taught Yang Luchan, the first non-clan member to learn the Chen family art.

skill in the past. China scholar Jarek Szymanski (2002) refers to Wu Wenhan's 吳文翰 book *"The Complete Book of the Essence and Applications of Wu (Yuxiang) 武禹襄 Style Taijiquan"* that contains a fascinating insight into the combat history of Chen style Taijiquan. It relates two official government documents that record the defence of Huaiqing County (where Chenjiagou is located) against the Taiping Rebellion army in 1853. One is entitled *"Veritable Record of Taiping Army Attacking Huaiqing County"*, which was written by Tian Guilin, who was responsible for "defending the western town" in Huaiqing. The other is the *"Daily Records of Huaiqing Defence"* compiled by a local schoolteacher called Ye Zhiji (Kennedy, 2005).

"Neither Tian nor Ye were Taijiquan practitioners. Both were government officials, and hence their accounts can be considered objective descriptions of the events". According to the documents, the Taiping army crossed the Yellow River and attacked Huaiqing County, the local militia was defeated and dispersed, and government troops escaped. Of all the villages only Chenjiagou resisted. In his "Veritable Record" under 29th day of the 5th month Tian Guilin noted:

Chen Zhongshen and Chen Jishen

"The head of the rebels called Big-Head Ram (Datou Yang) invaded Chenjiagou. This 'thief' was extremely bold and strong; he was able to carry two big cannons under his arms and swiftly attack the town. The battles which destroyed whole towns were conducted under the command of this thief. Fortunately Chen Zhongshen and Chen Jishen, two brothers from Chenjiagou, were very skilled in using spears and long poles. They used long poles to pull Big Head Ram down from the horse, and then they cut his head off. The rebels became very angry, and the whole group went on to Zhaobao Jie burning everything, then to Henei and villages around Baofeng, and no soldiers came to their rescue (of these areas, fortunately Chen Zhongshen and others managed to escape)".

The documents stated that only the inhabitants of Chenjiagou took an active part in the resistance against the Taiping rebels. This would imply that Chenjiagou, unlike the other villages in the area, had a stronger martial tradition and used it to defend themselves (Szymanski, 2002).

The Modern Era

During the early years of the last century Taijiquan practice in Chenjiagou reached its zenith, with almost everyone in the village training the art. At the same time, the establishment of a Taijiquan school and a more formalised teaching syllabus led to the development of many famous practitioners. In order to express their respect for the family art, the villagers re-constructed many of the dwellings of famous practitioners of the past and built many Taijiquan related structures (Wang Jie, 2006).

However, the good times were not to last and the fall of the Qing dynasty in 1912 brought a resurgence of regional warlordism to many parts of China, including Henan Province (Hucker, 1975). This period also saw much of China suffer a catalogue of devastating natural disasters. During the early 1920s much of Henan province, along with the neighbouring provinces of Shandong, Shanxi, Shaanxi and Hebei suffered a catastrophic period of famine caused by the severe droughts of 1919. In *The Search for Modern China*, Jonathan Spence (1999) described a shattered scene where:

"In farm villages ... the combination of withered crops and inadequate government relief was disastrous: at least 500,000 people died, and out of an estimated 48.8 million in these five provinces, over 19.8 million were declared destitute". Villagers were reduced to eating straw and leaves and epidemics such as typhus cut a swath through many too frail to fight back.

The disastrous combination of events led to the gradual exodus of the stronger and more able people from Chenjiagou in order to seek better conditions elsewhere. Taijiquan practice in the village declined. One of those to leave the village was Chen Fake 陈发科(1887-1957) of the seventeenth generation, who in 1928 went to Beijing to teach at the request of his nephew Chen Zhaopi 陈照丕. Travel was difficult in those days and Beijing must have seemed like the other side of the world to village people, most of whom would spend their entire lives in one place. One can imagine the sombre mood the night before he was to leave when Chen Fake went to the village temple to bid farewell to his fellow villagers and to demonstrate his Taijiquan skill one last time to the village elders.

Chen Fake devised the Xinjia or New Frame of Chen Taijiquan after settling in Beijing

Noted *Xiaojia* 小架 (Small Frame) practitioner Chen Liqing陈立清, a young child at the time, spoke of the incident: *"Chen Fake demonstrated Laojia Yilu. During the fajin* 发劲*movements you could feel the power from the wind and the flickers of candle-flames. At that time the temple was made of mud. When he stamped five of the roof tiles were dislodged and came down. One person tried to test his strength and was bounced off the wall. When he finished he saluted those present in the room"*. It was Chen Fake who devised the *Xinjia* or the New Frame of Chen Taijiquan after settling in Beijing.

In the later part of 1950s, Chen Zhaopi became deeply troubled that there would be no one left to transmit Taijiquan to the next generation in Chenjiagou, the birthplace of the system. He had left the village shortly before Chen Fake, teaching Chen Family Taiji throughout China including a period coaching at the prestigious Nanjing Martial Arts Academy. Chen Zhaopi was conscious that most of the capable teachers had left the village. He himself had learned from renowned clan masters including his uncles Chen Dengke陈登科, Chen Fake陈发科, and Chen Yanxi陈延熙 and Chen Xin陈鑫 of the previous generations. He was anxious that the young descendants of Chenjiagou would not miss the opportunity to continue their legacy. In 1958, the sixty-five year old Chen Zhaopi retired from work and returned to Chenjiagou to assume this daunting task.

Chen Zhaopi

To put the hardship and extreme poverty he faced into perspective one has only to consider that in the late 1950s and early 1960s an estimated twenty million Chinese people died as a result of Mao Zedong's disastrous economic policies. Chen Zhaopi's son, Chen Kesen陈克森 (1993) recalled his father's decision to pick up the mantle of preserving Taijiquan in its birthplace: *"He willingly returned to the spartan village life of Chenjiagou. After he returned to the village, he set up a Taijiquan school in his own home, bearing all of the costs himself. At the same time, he also set up a training class in the county town, Wenxian, teaching members of the government, the workers and the staff of the Mining School, and coaching the teachers and students. There was a vigorous renaissance of Taijiquan in old Wenxian. Who knew that this good scene would not last for long"?*

Chen Zhaopi set about improving and tightening the standard of Chen Style Tajiquan in the village, bringing under his tutelage many new devotees. The combination of his affectionate and easy-going nature and serious attitude to training attracted many students. The resurrection of the dwindling Chen family Taijiquan is generally attributed to this period of time. His most celebrated disciples today are Chen Xiaowang陈小旺, Wang Xian王西安, Zhu Tiancai朱天才 and Chen Zhenglei陈正雷, described collectively as the "Four Buddha's Warriors" by a journalist in the early 1980s. Reminiscing about this period, Chen Xiaowang (2005) remembered, *"at that time learning from my fifth uncle (Chen Zhaopi) was very grueling"*. The four young men were picked out among the ranks and were sent out to take part in various competitions and demonstrations, thus slowly increasing the profile of Chen style Taijiquan (Zhu Tiancai, 2000).

The Impact of the Cultural Revolution

In 1966 Mao Zedong and his close supporters instigated the Cultural Revolution, an immense and distorted movement that for ten years inflicted paranoia and anarchy on China. The Cultural Revolution was intended to transform China's society into one of equality, to wipe out the distinctions between the proletariat and the elite. However, by arousing peasant-powered mass violence, Mao let loose a whirlwind of social turmoil. Individuals deemed to be a *silei fenzi* 四类分子 or "four category elements"

In 1966 Mao Zedong instigated the Cultural Revolution, unleashing ten years of paranoia and anarchy on China.

were labelled as "bad class" and suffered severe discrimination. The four groups were defined as landlord, rich peasant, counter-revolutionary and rotten element. Throughout the countryside, anyone unlucky enough to be branded within these categories was shown little mercy in the highly-charged environment during the "Maoist struggle sessions". In *The Class System in Rural China: A Case Study*, Jonathan Unger (1984) documented the creation of caste-like pariah groups and their maltreatment during the post-revolutionary period. His study focused upon a small rural community in Guangdong province (coincidentally also called the Chen Village), which had many similarities to Chenjiagou. *"As a symbol of polluted status, during the 1960s and 1970s the dozen or so elderly 'four bad elements'…had to sweep dung from the village square before mass meetings were held there. To symbolise further that most of them were irredeemably among the damned, they were not permitted to attend any political sessions or participate in Mao study groups"*. At its heart, the Cultural Revolution demanded a comprehensive assault on the "four olds" within Chinese society: "old customs, old habits, old culture, and old thinking" (Spence, 1999).

Chen Bu's memorial stone

During the Cultural Revolution and the period of civil unrest just preceding it, many Taijiquan related structures in Chenjiagou were destroyed (Wang Jie, 2006). The tombstones of the Chen family were destroyed as the burial ground was turned into agricultural land. Chen Changxing's headstone was removed by a quick thinking villager who buried it until after the Cultural Revolution. Chen Bu's tombstone was also preserved (Chen Ziqiang, 2003). A number of priceless artifacts vanished, including Chen Wangting's sword, and a portrait of Chen Wanting with his disciple Jiang Fa 蒋发. Many historic Taijiquan documents were burnt. One story recounts how Wang Xian, one of the four 'Buddha's Warriors' was deeply upset to witness the

destruction of such irreplaceable manuscripts. Coming into possession of one such copy, he was determined that it be preserved and wrapped it in plastic and plastered it into the ceiling of his home. Discovery of his actions could have had dire consequences to himself and his family. Disastrously for the progress of Taijiquan in the village, many Taiji experts suffered greatly throughout this time.

The combination of incessant Maoist indoctrination and hard labour was the norm in villages all over China throughout the Cultural Revolution. Chen Xiaoxing陈小星, Principal of the Chenjiagou Taijiquan School today and nineteenth generation of the Chen Clan, recalled how he was required to toil for twelve hours a day in a brick factory. Chen Kesen recalled how his father, Chen Zhaopi, was persecuted and subjected to humiliating public "struggle sessions" during the Cultural Revolution, but courageously carried on teaching secretly at night. His dedicated disciples continued to study under him clandestinely, moving him to compose the following verse: *"At eighty years I teach Taiji, without concern for whether the road ahead is bad or good. The wind howls, the rain beats down and the difficulties are many; I delight in seeing the next generation of successors filling my home village"* (Chen Kesen, 1993). The severity of his persecution can be attested by his attempted suicide by jumping down a well.

In a radio interview conducted for the BBC Radio's Eastern Horizon programme in 2003, Chen Zhenglei explained: "The biggest setback for Taiji and all martial arts was during the Cultural Revolution when people were not able to practice freely and martial arts became outlawed. Taiji and other martial arts diminished in China. When China opened its gates again to the rest of the world, its rich culture was promoted and martial arts became standardised and simplified in the process. This has its pros and cons; it allows more people to learn Taiji, but ultimately dilutes and changes the virtues of the traditional form".

The Cultural Revolution ended in 1976 after the death of Mao Zedong and the arrest of its supporters and the political climate gradually improved. The outlook for Taijiquan in Chenjiagou also became brighter. Chen Zhaopi passed away in 1972 and now his disciples felt a pressing urgency to carry on what he had started. In 1974 Chen Zhaokui, the youngest son of Chen Fake (who left the village in 1928) was invited back to the village from Beijing to teach the X*injia 新架* (New Frame), the form devised by his father in the capital.

The village organised classes for all Chenjiagou villagers who wished to learn. Many of the villagers joined the classes and a small group was selected for intensive training, which included Chen Xiaowang, Zhu Tiancai, Wang Xian, Chen Zhenglei, Chen Dewang, Chen Lizhou, and others. Zhu Tiancai recounts how, "we would learn together in the public class in the mornings, then at night we would go for extra training. In the evenings, our teacher corrected each of our movements individually as we trained. Martial theories were taught and explained, and then we started to learn the Erlu 二路 and tuishou 推手 (push-hands). As we already had more than ten years of Laojia training experience behind us, we learned the 83-movement form very quickly, and in the process, also gained many new insights, deepening our understanding of Taijiquan".

In 1978, a host of new writings was given wide circulation through the state-controlled press and journals. "Focusing on the horrors and tragedies experienced by many in the Cultural Revolution, this "literature of the wounded" as it was called, stimulated debates and reflections about China's past and its future prospects. Signs seemed to point to a cultural thaw, among which one could include the convening of a conference (in far-off

Chen Zhoukui was invited to Chenjiagou to teach the New Frame devised by his father Chen Fake.

Kunming in Yunnan, admittedly) to study the long-taboo subject of comparative religion, with papers delivered on Buddhism and Daoism, Islam and Christianity" (Spence, 1999).

Taijiquan's rehabilitation was completed in 1978 when Deng Xiaoping 邓小平 in his position as Vice Chairman of the People's Republic of China wrote the simple words *"Taijiquan Hao* 太极拳好!*"* (Taijiquan is Good) for a group of visiting Japanese delegates. An article published in Chinese Wushu magazine (2003) under the title of *"Ten Significant Events in Wushu"* describes vividly the full impact of this statement: "Deng Xiaoping's writing breathed new life into the development of Taijiquan as well as other traditional Chinese martial arts. In the previous ten years all traditional arts had stagnated and were in danger of extinction. With the new China (after the Cultural Revolution) all the treasures of China were awaiting their fate. Nobody was certain whether the wide variety of martial arts would ever be able to see light again". Even though the political climate had eased, traditional martial arts were not a priority for the new legislation and were in a state of limbo. People lacked the confidence to practice openly and were waiting for a decision from higher up to revive it. "The very positive statement by Deng Xiaoping gave an indication to the whole of China that after the storm of the last ten years Taijiquan was going to enter a new era of regrowth". With the encouragement of these words martial arts very quickly began to bloom again as, once again, the old martial artists who had undergone immeasurable hardships picked themselves up and began to re-establish their arts.

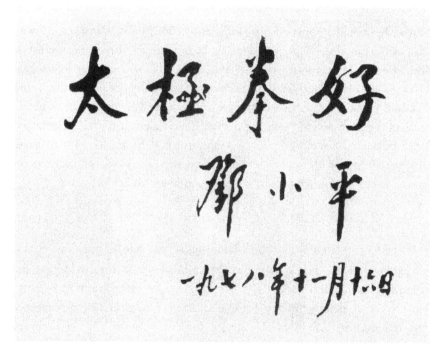

"Taijiquan is excellent". Deng Xiaoping's momentous calligraphy led to Taijiquan's emergence from the dark years of the Cultural Revolution.

Chenjiagou Today

To many, Taijiquan is synonymous with the more widely seen Yang style and the various government approved styles. However, in the last decades Chen style Taijiquan has enjoyed a surge of popularity around the world. As the current generation of Chenjiagou masters finally got the opportunity to travel and demonstrate their skills, more and more people have been exposed to the traditional village art. This has greatly broadened awareness of Chen Style Taijiquan and today Taiji practitioners from all over the world travel regularly to Chenjiagou in search of its root and to practice Chen Style Taijiquan at its birthplace.

Since the country opened its door and with the upsurge of China's economy, the district government is beginning to show an interest in Chenjiagou. It recognises that, as the birthplace of Taijiquan, the village carries with it profound cultural and historical significance not just in China, but the world over. Plans are afoot to develop Chenjiagou as a tourist attraction and in recent years the district government has invited architects from Beijing to survey and plan possible projects. So far the only officially designated tourist attractions in the village are the Taiji Temple and the house where Yang Luchan learned Taijiquan from Chen Changxing.

Twentieth generation inheritor Chen Bing陈炳, who is also the deputy village head at the time of writing, optimistically looks forward to the day when Chenjiagou and Taijiquan will go out into the international arena on a scale to match nearby Shaolin Temple. However, he provides the caveat of the requirement of higher-level government support: "If the central government takes an interest then the responsibilities placed upon the village towards its development will be much lighter. Individual influence is small; if you just rely on the villagers, teachers and instructors the development will be much smaller and slower. You need the infrastructure behind it, and at the moment the climate is favourable".

Today's favourable climate towards Chenjiagou was confirmed in June 2007 when the *People's Daily Overseas* newspaper reported that the birthplace of Taijiquan has been officially confirmed to be Wenxian County in Henan Province. The article reported on the findings of a multi-disciplinary group assembled by the Chinese People's Cultural Association to establish the origins of various Chinese cultural traditions. The group consisted of experts in the fields of Martial Arts, Culture and the Study of Antiquity. During the course of their investigations they conducted field research in Wenxian and concluded that the origins of Taijiquan can be traced to the area. The official report by Professor Kang Gewu 康戈武, Professor at the Chinese Wushu Research Institute and Secretary General of the Chinese Wushu Association, confirmed that this conclusion was reached after intensive research and examination, concurring with the findings of martial historian Tang Hao 唐豪 (1887-1959). On the morning of August 21st 2007 Feng Jianjun, the Deputy Head of the Chinese National Sports Association, unveiled a plaque in Chenjiagou to officially mark the village as the birthplace of Taijiquan.

Chenjiagou officially recognized as the birthplace of Taijiquan after the extensive research of the Chinese People's Cultural Association.

The Chenjiagou Taijiquan School

Village Economy

In May 2006 a team of eight students from the Henan Agricultural University Centre conducted a research study of Chenjiagou. They examined the pattern of employment and education of the villagers, as well as the village infrastructure and the position of the village economy today. The summary of their findings is thus:

Chenjiagou is still basically a farming community. The population is 2760 comprising some 600 families. Most of the people only receive primary education and university education is very rare. Many of the young people leave the village to go to various cities to seek unskilled work. The other group to leave the village for economic reasons are Taijiquan teachers. Most of them have gone out through invitations or introductions by friends to teach in various parts of China. The most famous teachers now teach abroad in different parts of the world.

Income in the village still comes mainly from agriculture.

Two modern twelve metre wide roads, constructed in 2003, run through the village from north to south and from east to west. The rest of the paths in the village were built in the 1980s and have fallen into disrepair. Because most of the paths are mud, transportation is very difficult during rainy times. The air in the village is comparatively good, as it has no heavy industry around the area to pollute it. Heating and cooking are mainly with coal and firewood, and most houses now have electricity and running water.

Income comes mainly from agriculture and outside employment. Wheat and maize are grown largely for personal consumption, as there is little surplus left over to sell. Crops planted for money include cotton, peanuts and melon. Also the four medicinal herbs, *tihuang*地黄 (Chinese fox-glove), *shanyao*山药 (mountain yam), *niujin*牛筋 (Dichotomanthus) and *juhua*菊花 (chrysanthemum), which are famous in this region.

Remembering the Ancestors

Throughout the village are various tombs, memorials and temples commemorating past generations of Taijiquan masters. In trying to understand their significance within the village, it is important not to appropriate them within a western scheme of values. Ancestor worship is among the most recognisable and well-known aspects of Chinese culture. From this standpoint, death does not represent the definitive end, but rather the progression of the spirit into a different plane of existence and a new state of being, and the continuation of the eternal natural cycle.

To chart the experience of generations of Taijiquan practitioners in Chenjiagou in any kind of meaningful way one must consider how they perceived the world. Chenjiagou, like many remote rural communities throughout the world, seems to give off a sense of timeless permanence. Each generation of the Chen clan preserved and built upon the family art passed down to them. The importance placed upon membership within a greater family provided individuals with a strong sense of identity. Including one's ancestors provide a sense of stability and permanence. Ancestor worship served to strengthen ties of kinship to the extent that within traditional Chinese social organisation, the concept of the patrilineal family was taken to be the essential cohesive unit of society. Blood kinship was and still is unquestionably the social tie of greatest significance.

Within traditional communities in China, the sense of genealogical descent carries with it a strong sense of belonging to a historical movement. Each member of the community is a vital part of an unbroken chain that links the living and the yet unborn with past generations of ancestors. While ancestors are believed to exist in another world after death, they continue to watch over their descendants. This relationship between the living and the dead is perceived as a dynamic two-way process. Ancestors are thought to assist those who care for them, and punish those who bring dishonour and injury to their kinsmen. In turn, the living must remember to care for the ancestors by venerating them on special occasions.

The Qingming Festival is one of the 24 seasonal division points in China. As well as marking the beginning of spring, it is a day of remembrance.

Communities such as Chenjiagou revere ancestors for a number of reasons. First, they are the founders of the family and therefore naturally have an interest in caring for it. They possess ancient knowledge and experience beyond that of the living; consequently it is commonplace to consult them for advice. Family members who bring honour and prosperity to the clan can expect to be rewarded with good health, fertility and success. Those who neglect their ancestors are liable to face failure, illness and poverty, as well as being shunned and ostracised by the community. The villagers of Chenjiagou trace their ancestry back to Chen Bu their historical patriarch.

To live beyond death is synonymous with being remembered and honoured by one's progeny. In contrast, to be forgotten is to enter a void as if one had never existed. For the most part, ancestors are remembered for three or four generations as their exploits are recalled and shrines honoured. Eventually, they join together under the universal category "Ancestors", which embraces all those that have gone before. A few outstanding ancestors, however, are remembered for many generations, their achievements in life being handed down in myths and folktales. Examples within the Chen clan include Chen Wangting, creator of Taijiquan; Chen Changxing, the fourteenth generation standard bearer who synthesized the Taijiquan forms of his predecessors into the routines still practiced today, as well as transmitting the family system outside the clan; Chen Fake, creator of the New Frame routines who took Chen Taijiquan out of the village to the capital Beijing; and Chen Zhaopi who resurrected Taijiquan in its birthplace.

To this day, all over China, traditional communities like Chenjiagou place the utmost importance on perpetuating the family line. A failure to produce children ultimately means that the ancestors are forgotten as the family dies out. As well as preserving the family line, the familial order of ancestor worship, to a large degree, incorporates and defines the roles of both the living and the dead. Within the Chen family, this sense of obligation is extended to the propagation of the family skill in Taijiquan. Speaking to the current generation of masters to emerge from Chenjiagou there is a recurring sentiment of not wanting to be seen as the one who failed to preserve the family's legacy after so many unbroken generations.

Chen Zhaopi's memorial garden in Chenjiagou

The secrecy of the rural family clans is one important reason why many family martial systems were able to develop their own unique characteristics and flavour. The patriarchal clan system was an essential condition for the development of many distinctive local combat systems. The great importance traditionally placed in the family, it's strict isolation from other clans and its autonomous way of life preserved many rural martial styles over generations. Outsiders were granted no access to this knowledge.

The Confucian worldview did emphatically state that social stability was dependent upon a strict hierarchic ordering in human relations. As mentioned above, Chinese religious thinking contained ideas of collective justice through the patrilineage; family members suffering ill fortune were frequently believed to be paying for the wrongdoings of their parents or grandparents. On a more sinister level, the notion of collective legal guilt has been widely applied throughout Chinese history. In imperial law, punishments for the most serious offences could extend to the family of the perpetrator, sometimes including even distant relations. These traditional notions of social order and of collective religious and legal guilt were still evident in rural thought during the 1960s (Watson, 1984).

Paying respect to generations past. Ancestor worship gives a palpable sense of belonging to an unbroken kinship chain. With it comes both the comfort of knowing that the ancestors are watching out for those that remember them and the responsibility of bringing honour to the clan.

CHAPTER TWO

RETURNING TO THE SOURCE

The writings of Confucius (above) alongside Daoist and Buddhist teachings emphasise balance and harmony and shape Chinese culture.

Philosophical Roots

The Chinese orientation towards life is shaped by the blending of three philosophies: Daoism, Confucianism and Buddhism. Each philosophy emphasises harmony, and largely discourages the abstract speculation common in the West. An occidental student of Taijiquan usually approaches Taijiquan with a mind coloured by a different philosophical core. The way he thinks is largely inherited from the Greek, Jewish and Christian patterns of analysis that are two thousand or more years old.

To fully understand Taijiquan it is necessary to understand its underlying philosophy, the Taiji theory. This does not pose too great a problem for Chinese students, as many of the ideas are omnipresent throughout their everyday culture. Occidental students, however, need to explore aspects of Chinese thought that have permeated its culture for several thousand years. Failure to grasp the philosophy results in one training a superficial system that is lacking in real foundation: The great 18th generation exponent Chen

Zhaopi 陈照丕 believed that this does not just apply to Taijiquan, but that every action a person undertakes in everyday life should be in harmony with a higher philosophy.

The Taiji Theory
Yin and Yang

"One producing two is a spontaneous principle. Change is the alternation of Yin and Yang. The supreme ultimate [Taiji] is their principle"

Zhu Xi's 朱熹 commentary on the Yijing

Taijiquan is the 'Fist of Taiji', denoting the adaptation of taji principles into a martial arts form. The core ideology of the *Yijing* 易经 - 'The Book of Changes' - provides the bedrock upon which the theory of Taiji is based. Wang Zongyue 王宗岳 (1736-1796), the renowned Taijiquan theorist wrote: *"Taiji 太极 is borne from wuji 无极. It is the generator of movement and stillness. It is the mother of yin and yang. When it moves it divides and at rest it reunites"*. Wuji is described in the *Yijing* as the insubstantial emptiness or a minute point of space. Through Taiji's pivotal action the two polarities *(Liang Yi 两仪)* of yin and yang are created and from the two polarities it is believed that all things are born. The two polarities divide again into Four Phases *(Si Xiang 四象)* and the Four Phases into Eight Trigrams *(Ba Gua 八卦)*, and from the Eight Trigrams Sixty-Four Hexagrams are derived and so on until millions of objects are produced, hence the phrase: *"one yin one yang is the dao 道"*. The dynamic interchange of the two opposite polarities is thus used to understand everything within the natural world, or to *"view ten thousand things"*. Moving in endless cycles has long been considered to be the basic pattern of movement of the *dao*. *"The natural pivotal function of movement and stillness is called the 'dao' 道, or the 'law (li 理) of great nature"*. *"Those who practice Taijiquan must know yin and Yang. To know yin and yang, one must know the meaning of Taiji"*. (Wang Zongyue).

In Chinese culture and philosophy it has come to be an all-embracing concept: Yin is linked with darkness, cold, contraction, water, inactivity, femininity and matter. Yang conversely corresponds to brightness, heat, expansion, fire, activity, masculinity and energy. These apparently opposing aspects are really two sides of the same coin. Each cannot be understood except in relation to the other - like the attraction between positive and negative electrical forces. *"The sky is yang and the earth is yin; mountain is yang and water is yin; male is yang and female yin. In a nutshell, everything in the universe is yin and yang. Without the theory of yin and yang the world does not exist as everything is comparative".*

Chen Wangting 陈王庭, the creator of Taijiquan, used this precept as the basis for his unique martial art. Taiji's yin and yang theory is the foundation of the entire Taijiquan system. It is characterised by the co-existence of both aspects in all its entirety, internally from the yang emotional mind *(xin*心*)* and the yin logical mind *(yi*意*)* to externally the combination of hardness and softness, opening and closing, solidity and emptiness, bending and extending, retreating and advancing, withdrawing and releasing, and the alternation of fast and slow movements, etc. Each of these combine and interchange to make the apparent contradiction become complementary and, in the process, forming the Taiji principle of balance and alternation.

Chen Zhaopi wrote: *"The core precept of Taijiquan is gang*刚 *(hardness) and rou*柔 *(softness)"* and gave the examples – *"movement is gang, stillness is rou; opening is gang, closing is rou; releasing power is gang, gathering energy is rou; jin is gang and qi is rou. Therefore gang-rou is Taiji is yin-yang and within Taiji yin and yang are inseparable. The concept of yin-yang exists throughout the universe and also throughout Taijiquan".* The Taijiquan player must seek a state of balance being neither deficient nor excessive in terms of yin and yang. Ultimately, the skilled exponent achieves a balance of the external physical body and the internal visceral body. In practical terms, this is embodied by optimum body alignment, increased physical strength and the ability to maintain the body's equilibrium at all times. At its heart is the idea of wholeness, progression and balance.

The Essence of Taijiquan 太極之粹

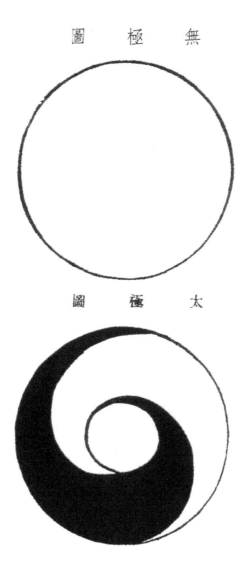

Diagrams from Chen Xin's *Illustrated Explanation of Chen Family Taijiquan* showing *Wuji* (above) and *Liang Yi* – Taiji's dual polarities of Yin and Yang.

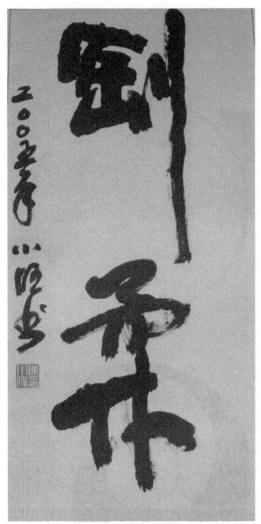

"Gang Rou" Calligraphy by Chen Xiaowang

"The core precept of Taijiquan is gang (hardness) and rou (softness)… movement is gang, stillness is rou; opening is gang, closing is rou; releasing power is gang, gathering energy is rou; jin is gang and qi is rou".

Chen Zhaopi

The Essence of Taijiquan 太極之粹

The Eight Trigrams

As a medium for the imaginative association of ideas the eight trigrams (*bagua*), espoused in the *Yijing* has provided a theoretical framework for much great life wisdom through the ages. In *Navigating Through Chaos in China* (2006), Ronny Julius C. said that: *"The Book of Changes provides in the first place a tool. It is an early version of Microsoft's Windows, with yin-yang inside. It is a tool that helps to organise views and helps to arrange views…"*.

The basic symbols are the broken (- -) and unbroken (—) lines, which combine into eight permutations of trigrams and sixty-four sets of hexagrams – each made up of a grouping of two trigrams. The broken line symbol represents yin and the unbroken line symbol represents yang and is known as *Liang Yi* 兩儀 (Two Polarities). The Four Phases *(Si Xiang* 四象*)* are the result of the combination of the two polarities, for example, the placing of two yang symbols one above the other (two unbroken lines), to denote Greater Yang. Three layers of yin-yang symbols are known as the Trigrams and are the maximum number of figures that can be formed from the two line symbols. The Eight Trigrams *(Bagua* 八卦*)*, derived from the division of the four phases, are used to classify all phenomena and to analyse them by searching for the mutual relationships of their principles.

Taijiquan has adopted these basic principles and often uses the Trigrams to illustrate its principles. For instance, the inner trigrams represent one's state of mind and the outer trigrams the external requirements of the body. The Eight external Trigrams have also come to represent the eight intrinsic energies, or Eight Gates *(Ba Men* 八門*)* of Taijiquan, as they are concerned with the eight directions of combat in Taijiquan. The primary energies *peng, lu, ji, an* 掤, 捋, 擠, 按 (warding, diverting, squeezing, pressing) are matched with the four main directions *kan, zhen, li* and *dui*, while the secondary energies of *cai, lie, zhou, kao* 采、挒、肘、靠 (plucking, splitting, elbowing, bumping) are matched with the four diagonal directions, *qian, gen, xun* and *kun* 乾艮巽坤 (see table on page 64)

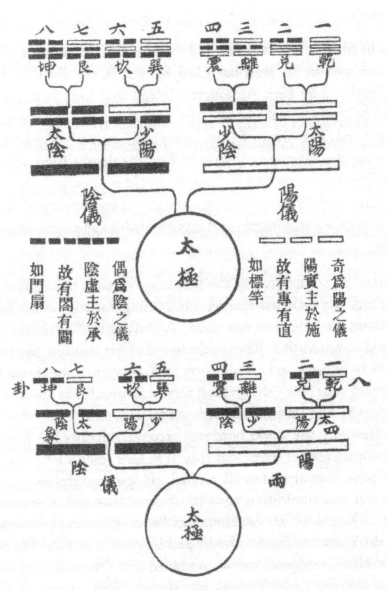

Image from Chen Xin's *Illustrated Explanation of Chen Family Taijiquan*. The Two Polarities (*Liang Yi*) divide into our Phases (*Si Xiang*) and the Four Phases into Eight trigrams (*Ba Gua*).

NORTH	KAN	坎	PENG 掤
EAST	ZHEN	震	LU 捋
SOUTH	LI	离	JI 挤
WEST	DUI	兑	AN 按
NORTH-WEST	QIAN	乾	CAI 采
NORTH-EAST	GEN	艮	LIE 挒
SOUTH-EAST	XUN	巽	ZHOU 肘
SOUTH-WEST	KUN	坤	KAO 靠

The Eight Trigrams according to the sequence of King Wen.

Together with the Five Elements *(Wuxing 五行)* of Taijiquan movements, this has become collectively known as the 'thirteen postures' of Taijiquan.

Five Elements

The Five Elements have been closely connected to yin-yang theory since the Han dynasty. Five-element theory presupposes a dynamic cycle of metal, wood, water, fire, and earth, each enjoying ascendancy over its predecessor. Sinologist Joseph Needham explained that through natural observation Chinese thinkers had formulated a theory of "mutual conquest": wood (or vegetation) overcomes earth by drawing its sustenance from it; metal overcomes wood, for instance via the use of an axe to fell trees; fire melts metal; water extinguishes fire; and earth overcomes water by absorbing it. For centuries it has been used as a system of ordering and classifying the relationship between all things and the inter-relationships of natural and human forces. Chinese cosmologists believed that by discovering the appropriate "machinery" for aligning the human realm with the realm of nature their ability to control the human world was greatly enhanced (Schwartz, 1985).

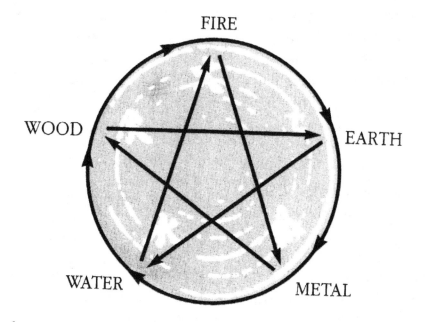

The Essence of Taijiquan 太極之粹

Chen Xin – Chen Taijiquan theorist

Chen Family Taijiquan utilises the theory of five elements, categorised in the conventional order: metal (*jin*金); wood (*mu*木); water (*shui*水); fire (*huo*火); and earth (*tu*土) as a basis for its actions of advance, retreat, guard the left, anticipate the right and the position of central equilibrium (*zhong ding*中定). Chen Xin陈鑫 wrote: "*The doctrine of creation and destruction allocated to the Five Elements embraces all things under heaven. In hand-to-hand combat, the weaker fighters are associated with yin. The yin substance that is able to destroy yang corresponds with water. Water can destroy fire in accordance with the doctrine of the Five Elements…*". Also, "*…during an opponent's smooth and soft advance, one suddenly replaces soft with a hard counter-attack, resembling water transforming into wood*".

Chen Zhaopi gave some examples to illustrate the theory within the handform:

Metal corresponds to the west. In the handform it is represented by advancing actions such as *Lou Xi Ao Bu* 搂膝坳步 (Embrace Knee and Stepping Obliquely).

Wood corresponds to the east and denotes actions that move backwards, for instance *Dao Juan Hong* 倒卷宏 (Stepping Back and Whirling Arms).

Water is linked to the north. In the handform, this element equates to the movement *Yun Shou* 云手 (Cloud Hands) when the left hand is pushing out and the practitioner is watching the left side.

Fire is correlated to the south direction. In the handform, this element again equates to the movement *Yun Shou* 云手 (Cloud Hands) but this time when the right hand is pushing out and the practitioner is "anticipating" the right side.

Earth is associated with the centrally balanced or *zhong ding* 中定 position. Examples in the handform include postures like *Dan Bian* 单鞭 (single Whip) and the finishing position of *Xie Xing* 斜行 (Oblique Step).

The Essence of Taijiquan太極之粹

Davidine Siaw-Voon Sim in Dan Bian, a posture said by Chen Zhaopi to reflect the Earth element.

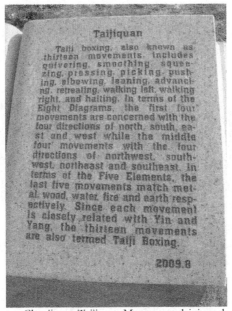

Stone tablet in the new Chenjiagou Taijiquan Museum explaining why *Taiji Boxing* is also referred to as the *"13 Movements"*.

The 13 postures of Taijiquan

The *"Thirteen Postures of Taijiquan"* has several interpretations. Philosophically, the thirteen postures are based on the arrangements of the Eight Trigrams (*Bagua*八卦) and Five Elements (*Wuxing*五行), whose numbers add up to thirteen. All Taijiquan styles list eight fundamental energies or techniques: *Peng, Lu, Ji, An, Cai, Lie, Zhou* and *Kao* 掤,捋,挤,按,采,挒、肘、靠. Chen style Taijiquan exponents also include the additional five techniques: *Teng, Shan, Zhe, Kong* and *Huo* 腾,闪,折,空,活, These can be broadly divided into three categories of four techniques, and one all-encompassing quality. (See table on the following page).

In the study of Taijiquan's *neijin*內勁, Chen Zhaopi listed thirteen features of Chen Family Taijiquan as: *zhan*粘 (stick), *you*游 (flow), lian连 (connect), *sui*随 (follow), *teng* 腾(leap), *shan*闪 (dodge), *zhe*折 (return), *kong*空 (empty), *peng* 掤(ward off), *lu* 捋(divert), *ji* 挤(squeeze), *an* 按(press), and *huo*活 (flexible/lively).

Frontal methods:	Peng 掤	Supporting energy characterised by a feeling of buoyancy and outward expansion
	Lu 捋	Diverting either upwards or downwards in an oblique drawing action
	Ji 挤	A crowding force that is a deliberate attempt to compress an opponent
	An 按	Applying pressure or pushing that is powered by weight
Diagonal Methods:	Cai 采	A combination of rotating, pressing and closing downwards.
	Lie 挒	Split using two opposing forces
	Zhou 肘	Striking with the elbows
	Kao 靠	Short range strike with any part of the body
Additional Dynamic Methods	Teng 腾	Leaping to facilitate an attack or defence
	Shan 閃	Rapid dodging, often used as a strategic manoeuvre
	Zhe 折	Folding
	Kong 空	Becoming empty; a leading in or neutralising method
To remain within the principle	Huo 活	To remain flexible and lively (literally to be alive)

As well as the eight fundamental energies common to all Taijiquan styles, Chen style Taijiquan also includes the additional five techniques: *Teng, Shan, Zhe, Kong* and *Huo*.

Daoism and Taijiquan

Daoism provides many of the underpinnings of Chinese thinking, which so differentiates it from the West. Specifically, there are the concepts of balance and paradox: many examples are immediately applicable to Taijiquan, *"Heavy is the root of light; calm is the ruler of haste; yield and overcome etc."* (Feng and English, 1973). Daoist thinking holds that nature is as it is and that within the cosmos everything has its natural place and function. This can only be distorted and misunderstood when it is defined, labelled, or evaluated. *"The object of human wisdom is to fall in line with the Dao or the ways and laws of nature and live in harmony with them"* (Lin Yutang, 1951). Trying too hard is the surest way not to achieve - for example the Taijiquan practitioner who makes the mistake of "trying" to relax instead of just relaxing. Generations of teachers have instructed their students to practice according to the correct principles and let nature take its course.

Chen Zhaokui 陈照奎 illustrated this unhurried approach when recounting a story of two prospective students who wished to study with his father Chen Fake 陈发科. The first had already practiced martial arts for a number of years, a point he was quick to make known to his potential teacher. He then enquired how long it would take for him to reach a high level of skill. Chen Fake replied with his usual answer to this question, *"in three years expect small success, in five years expect medium success and great success in ten years"*. On hearing this, the first student responded brashly that he would train one hundred times harder than his classmates and achieve excellence within a year.

The second student, after expressing his desire to join the class, quietly stated that he would try his best for as long as the teacher felt necessary. Speaking to his class later, Chen Fake observed that the impatience of the first student would inhibit his learning, as his mind was not calm but filled with his own experiences and expectations. The second student's open mind meant that he would fare better and could expect to make good

Chen Family Temple mural of Laozi – originator of Daoist philosophy.

progress. Approaching the learning process with an attitude unclouded by past experiences and assumptions, the skill can be absorbed naturally over time. This is the opposite of the aforementioned idea of an individual "trying to relax". Instead, the process of mind-body relaxation occurs in a natural and inevitable sequence – as the mind relaxes the emotions become calm and the body begins to relax.

Ultimately Daoism teaches the importance of *wu-wei* 无为, a term that is often translated simplistically as 'non-action'. The term does not mean doing nothing, which implies languor and lack of thought, but rather to not indulge in useless or unnecessary effort and to not do anything that contradicts nature. What is asked of the skilled Taijiquan exponent is the honing of a kind of unpremeditated, non-deliberative, non-calculating and non-purposive response. In *The Taoist Body*, Kristofer Schipper (1996) suggested that to go against the principle of *wu-wei* by intervening: *"means in effect to violate nature by going against the spontaneous process with actions inspired and influenced by our partial view of things. Imbalance results from this intervention".*

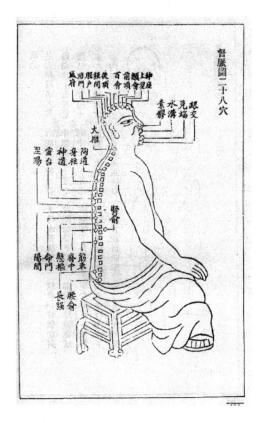

Qi – The Power Source of Taijiquan

"...one's will (zhi志) and consciousness (yi意) determine the development of qi and its transformation into spirit (shen神)"
– Chen Xin

Taijiquan is a sophisticated system that combines traditional *wushu* 武术 (martial arts), *daoyin tuna* 导引吐纳 (the ancient methods of leading and guiding energy allied to the science of breathing) and Chinese medical theory. To gain an accurate understanding of the discipline one must consider each of these aspects.

The conventional Western analysis of the human body stresses the physical structures and components that act together in a very subtle and complex way. Using the science of anatomy and physiology these structures are charted from the largest – bones, muscles, skin, etc – to the microscopic level of cells and their components. This structural map underpins the basic model of cause and effect that is prevalent in the Western understanding of how the body works.

The Chinese model is radically different. For thousands of years the components of process, rather than the physical body structure, is considered as more important. The human body is viewed primarily as an energy system within which a variety of substances interact in a dynamic manner to produce the whole physical organism. These essential elements include blood, body fluids and also qi 气 *(vital energy)*, jing 精 *(fundamental essence of life)*, shen 神 *(the spirit)*.

Understanding the Concept of Qi

The concept of *qi* 气 (pronounced: "chee" and often written as chi) in the Chinese language is imbued with many different layers of meaning. Translating the word qi across the barriers of culture and time presents a formidable challenge to modern day Taijiquan enthusiasts. Variously translated as "energy", "vital energy" or "life force", there is no satisfactory word-for-word equivalent in the English language for qi.

To understand fully the teachings of past generations of Taijiquan masters it is essential to analyse concepts such as qi reflectively and take into account their cultural context. While it may be difficult for Western practitioners to get to grips with ancient Chinese ideas like qi, it is nonetheless a worthwhile quest. Deciphering the thoughts of past teachers such as Chen Xin, the most famous Chen Taijiquan theorist, certainly has barriers of language, history and culture. However, it has the shared world of physical experience to draw upon. Ultimately, one of the best ways to try to understand qi is by being aware of what it does.

The conventional Chinese understanding of qi embraced a number of different characteristics. In everyday speech, it refers to the fresh air, the breath, any gaseous matters, smells etc. It also refers to feelings and the emotions, and to manner, morale and spirit. The two Chinese characters that comprise the ideogram for qi 氣 represents "vapour" or "steam", and" uncooked rice" or "grain". The steam that rises from the cooking rice corresponds to qi in an unformed state, while the rice symbolises the substantial and material aspect of matter. *"Inherent in the Chinese word is the transformative and changing essence of qi from the material to the immaterial and back again"* (Xiaolan Zhao, 2006).

Philosophically it was often applied to explain sensation and awareness, both existing and potential. At the end of the Ming and beginning of the Qing dynasty, the time when Chen Wangting created Taijiquan, Fang Yizhi方以智, in his work, *A little Understanding of the Principles of Things*, discussed the nature and subtleness of qi in a series of subtle texts on the natural sciences:

"The world has only to grasp a form and it is apparent, yet qi is subtle. As in winter when breath comes out of the mouth one's qi is like smoke. If a person stands in direct sunlight, a haze rises above his head and its shadow is seen on the earth…it fills up all spaces, threads through all substances."

In a seventeenth century essay entitled *"The Mechanism of Rest"*, Chang Nai spoke of a system of "vital energy" upon which human life was entirely dependent. Chang used the example of plants, where the flowers and fruit grow above the earth while the roots are buried below. An unseen energy continuously circulates between the roots and flowers without which growth and restoration are not possible. The parallels with Chen Wangting's new art are immediately apparent, as illustrated by the Taiji saying that states that if one *"cultivate the roots, the leaves will be abundant"*. Another practical comparison offered for this vital energy is the act of covering up a brazier with hot ashes. Outwardly at rest, the fire continues, ready to burst into flame the moment firewood is added (Lin Yutang, 1963).

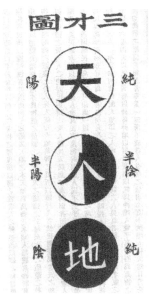

Illustration from Chen Xin's canon: heaven above, earth below, man balanced in the centre.

According to Chinese medical theory, qi is a substance that is perpetually moving and energy producing. It is held to be the most fundamental substance that is needed within the body to maintain life. Those with a strong constitution are thought to possess an abundance of this vital force, hence their bodies are strong and they can anticipate a long healthy life. In contrast those with a weak constitution are held to be lacking in this area and can expect to suffer poor health and a shortened lifespan. Qi was believed to be a basic elemental component of the universe; it is a matter that flowed through all things animate and inanimate.

Ancient Chinese philosophers believed that the heavens and the earth were formed from the original qi. At the beginning of the world the more refined, quintessential qi rose up to form the heavens, whereas the impure heavy qi sank, congealed and produced the Earth. Within the human body it flowed, like the blood, via a series of channels to the extremities. The blockage or leakage of this vital energy was believed to be the cause of many diseases. Because qi is believed to be such an important substance, it has always been elevated onto a pedestal. For centuries it has been viewed a life force to be guarded carefully lest its stores be depleted. Consequently, generations of health promoters and martial artists have emphasised the cultivation and the storage of this vital life force.

So how does all this talk about qi help Taijiquan practitioners to increase their skill and the quality of their health in a practical way? To begin with, one must have some understanding of the traditional Chinese classification of qi is and its origin. There are three sources of qi:

- *Yuan qi* 元气, meaning original qi, is also known as primordial qi. This refers to the qi that an individual is born with and is considered to be an inheritance from his/her parents. The quality of *yuan qi* varies from person to person and makes up an individual's constitution and determines his/her propensity towards health or disease. After birth, *yuan qi* is stored in the kidneys. Its function is to initiate and promote the vital activities, i.e. the growth and development of the human body, and the functional activities of the internal organs.

- *Gu qi* 榖气, meaning grain qi, is generated by the food one takes after birth and is distributed all over the body to produce nutrients, blood and energy under the action of the spleen and stomach. Its chief function is to nourish the physique of the body.

- *Kong qi* 空气 is derived from the fresh air inhaled by the lungs after birth and is the main source of qi of the human body.

Gu qi and *kong qi* are acquired through the consumption of healthy food and breathing good air. However the congenital *Yuan qi*, which determines the growth and development of the human body, gradually declines as a person grows older. Therefore it needs to be supplemented through specific cultivation.

The Essence of Taijiquan 太極之粹

"Qi" – calligraphy by Zhu Tiancai

Yuan qi determines the growth and development of the human body and gradually declines as a person gets older.

The processes by which qi works in the body is a challenging study in its own right. To illustrate, *gu qi* and *kong qi* are said to combine to form *zong qi* 宗气 *(gathering qi);* the *zong qi* is catalysed by the action of the *yuan qi* to form *zhen qi* 真气 (true qi), which becomes the qi that circulates through the channels and organs of the body. The circulation of *zhen qi* underpins a number of bodily functions. *Zhen qi* provides the source of nutritive qi *(ying qi* 营气*)*, which is necessary in the process of nourishing the tissues within the body. In addition, it forms the basis of defensive qi *(wei qi* 卫气*)* that flows around the outside of the body guarding it from external pathogens that could potentially give rise to disharmony and illnesses. *"When the zhen qi flows through each of the various internal organs of the body, the qi functions with respect to the characteristics of that organ. Thus, for example, the activity of liver qi will be different from that of lung qi, but they are both manifestations of zhen qi. Similarly, when zhen qi flows through the channels or meridians of the body it is called meridian qi (jingluo zhi qi* 经络之气*)"* (Williams, 1996). The terminology is complex, but basically what is being described is the process by which the food that we eat and the air that we breathe are metabolised internally, to produce the qi that flows through the meridians, and the qi that flows outside of the meridians as protection.

Mural of Chen Zhaopi in the Chen Family Temple

On Internal Training

In his teaching notes, 18th generation Chen master Chen Zhaopi gave a guideline on the importance of internal training. He first emphasised training qi, stating that *"everything culminates in one breath of qi"*. In order to decipher the content of Chen Zhaopi's teaching, it is useful to briefly explain the basic mechanism of qi movement in accordance with Chinese medical theories:

The movements of qi can be classified into four aspects: ascending, descending, entering and exiting, which are based on directions. Entry, exit, ascending and descending movements of qi must be kept in harmony and the two opposite aspects should be balanced. A free flow of qi as well as balancing the ascent, descent, and exit and entry movements of qi is known as the harmony of activities of qi.

Disharmony of the activities of qi ensues if balance is broken. This commonly consists of five states: adverse upward flow of qi; collapse of qi; escape of qi; obstruction of qi in its outward flow, stagnation of qi. The adverse upward flow of qi refers to excessive ascent or insufficient descent of qi. When the pathway for descent is obstructed, qi goes upward instead. Collapse of qi results mostly from excessive descent or inadequate ascent of qi. Escape of qi indicates the inability of qi to be kept within the body, which leads to loss of qi. Obstruction of qi in is usually caused by obstruction in the pathways for qi in the interior of the body to go outwards. Stagnation of qi, means that there is an impeded flow of qi in the whole body or in a local area.

Bearing in mind qi describes an energy as well as a feeling, Chen Zhaopi identified five 'refined' qi and five 'bad' or unbalanced qi. Training should be approached with the aim of eliminating the five negative qi while cultivating five beneficial types of qi. He maintained that one can only perceive and appreciate qi though its outward manifestation and through its effectiveness.

'Bad' qi to be trained out of the body are:

Heng Qi 横气 (*heng* translates as traverse) is experienced as a feeling of tightness across the chest. He explained it as qi accumulating in the chest (instead of up and down) so that one's breath (respiration) cannot connect smoothly. During exercises the breathing quickly becomes laboured and panting occurs.

Xie Qi 邪气 (*xie* means deviant) occurs when breathing has not yet been correctly regulated. While practicing Taijiquan, the individual is able to coordinate breathing with the movements only intermittently and sometimes holds the breath. A common symptom of *xie qi* is pallor and "green lips" after exercise.

Zhi Qi 滞气 *(zhi* means stagnant*)* is when the *zhong qi* 中气 (centralised essential energy that flows up and down the vertical axis of the upper and lower body) is blocked and qi therefore cannot circulate through the body. One should try to correct this before it becomes chronic with consequences to one's strength and health.

Ni Qi 逆气 *(ni* means adverse). An example of this is when the shoulders are lifted and elbows are up. This is manifested when the practitioner does not know how to relax the shoulders and sink the elbows (*song jian chen zhou* 松肩沉肘). *Ni qi* interrupts and reverses the flow of *zhong qi* and can thus lead to illnesses.

Zhuo Qi 浊气 *(zhuo* translates as opaque*)* occurs where the Taijiquan player has not learned how to relax and loosen the upper body whilst sinking and making the lower body heavy and stable. This person tends to be top heavy and relies entirely on external strength. The external forms are dispersed and the internal form is empty. When opaque energy is raised all the time, a person will suffer from ill health.

The five types of refined qi to be cultivated are:

Xiantianziran Zhi Qi 先天自然之气 (Prenatal Qi). This is the intrinsic energy one is born with. It determines the nature of internal resources conferred on an individual. Taijiquan practice builds and maintains this internal resource.

Qiankun Zheng Qi 乾坤正气 (Universal Refined Qi) is also known as *Yin-Yang Qi* and also as *Gang Rou* (Hard-Soft) *Qi*. This energy is generated through stringent practice so that opposing aspects of qi can be balanced and the whole body becomes integrated and harmonised.

Taihe Zhi Qi 太和之气 (Supreme Harmony Qi) is Dantian Qi. *It* combines the qi of the five internal organs - heart, liver, spleen, lungs and kidneys - and is often referred to in older Chinese texts as *"wu qi chao yuan* 五气朝元*"* or *"five qi returns to origin"*. In traditional Chinese medicine the quality of the original (*yuan*) qi determines the seriousness and the likely prognosis of a patient's illness

Haoran Zhi Qi 浩然之气 (Grand Refined Energy). Qi, led by the consciousness, descends downward to stabilise the lower body, leaving the upper body light and agile. When *haoran zhi qi* is refined, the body's energy is patent and unimpeded, the practitioner breathes comfortably, speaks naturally, and does not pant. The facial colour remains unchanged, even after very strenuous exercises. With this level of attainment, Chen Zhaopi says *"in combat one can face an opponent calmly"*.

Hunyuan Yi Qi 混元一气 (Transmuted Unified Qi) is realised when the practitioner's gongfu is complete to the point when the whole body's energy is fortified and concentrated. "*Hunyuan yi qi* is solid as metal, impenetrable when attacked and does not disperse when invaded".

Therefore one must train to dispel the five adulterated qi and absorb the five types of refined qi. Trapped qi are stagnant energy, whereas qi that descend into the dantian are refined energy. During practice, allow the impure qi to sink right down to the *yongquan* acupoint, and rise up to the *baihui* acupoint. In this way "one can not only make the muscles and bones stronger, but also keep illnesses at bay and increase one's life span".

Yun Qi 运气 – Directing Qi

Qi is a central concept of many oriental martial arts, which use myriad training methods to train it. Chen Zhaopi, however, suggested that training qi *(lien qi* 练气*)* can essentially be divided into three approaches, all of which can help to maintain health, make one less susceptible to illness and strengthen the body's constitution.

"*Yong qi* 用气" (using qi) is the method of training the whole body to be physically very strong so that more force can be delivered in order to meet incoming energy. This is generally favoured by the *waijiaquan* 外家拳 or external martial arts. A second approach is "*yang qi* 养气" or cultivating qi. Using exercises such as sitting meditation, the body is trained to accumulate qi so that it is not dispersed and scattered. Finally, there is "*yun qi* 运气" or circulating and directing energy, where the body's energy is trained to become contained and wholesome and then directed to the extremities and to the rest of the body. Chen Zhaopi said that once this is realised *"one will be able to intercept and borrow incoming strength and to return it (jie li da ren* 借力打人*); this is gongfu and is the essence of Taijiquan".*

The importance of *yun qi* in Taijiquan is encapsulated in the saying: *"If qi is not rooted in the body, one appears soft but has no substance; if cannot be expressed in the four extremities, one appears strong but is weak"* 气不本于身则虚而不实，不行于四梢则实而入虚": 'Appears soft but has no substance' in this case refers to the result of the inability to generate energy (and power) from the dantian. Movements may be exact and aesthetic but *"when qi is not generated from the dantian, the person is merely moving the arms and legs. The qi has no basis, like a river without source".* Training will result in few health benefits and the practitioner will not be able to successfully apply any technique in a combat situation.

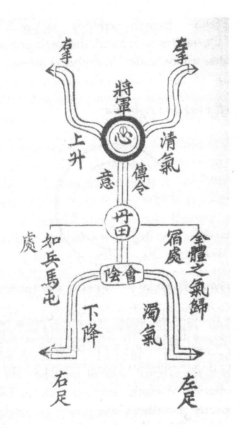

Chen Xin's illustration of qi circulation throughout the body.

However, it is also necessary to be able to bring one's energy to the extremities so that it can be used. *'Appearing strong but is weak'* refers to an inability to transmit energy to the four extremities. Travelling from the root to the fringe, energy has its source in the dantian, but its destination varies depending upon the posture being assumed and the techniques being used. Taijiquan requires this constant circulation of energy from the dantian out through the four limbs to the extremities before returning to the dantian.

An often-quoted Taijiquan saying is: *"if your hand arrives but your body doesn't arrive, you will not overcome your foe* 手到身不到, 击敌不得妙". To perform Taijiquan effectively the external shape must be led by the internal energy (*neiqi* 内气) from the dantian. In practice, movement by any part of the body must move from the inside out, from the root to the extremity in order to achieve integrated whole body movement. Chen Zhaopi refers to this as *"wanzheng yiqi完整一气"*, which translates as *"one complete qi"*. When a practitioner reaches a level of skill whereby he can freely use integrated whole body movements he manifests *"the hand and the body arrive together, ridding the foe like pulling out weeds手到身也到，击敌如摧草"* as described in the boxing canon. Also, *"A river fed by a source will flow continuously, and a tree with deep roots will produce copious branches and foliage如水有源，便滔滔不断，木有本便枝叶茂盛"*.

When the old texts refer to the extremities it is important to be clear about what they actually mean. A simplistic assumption would lead one to think only of the head, the hands and the feet, the terminus of the external body. The old masters often refer to the extremities as being extended to encompass the blood, the tongue, teeth and nails.

Reaching the *'extremity of the blood'* refers to energy reaching the limits of where the blood flows (i.e. to the furthest reaches of the capillary network). In Traditional Chinese Medicine blood is not considered only as the physical substance recognised in Western medicine. It is viewed as a material and liquid manifestation of qi that serves to nourish the body and spirit (*shen*神). Continuously circulating throughout the body, blood carries the nutritive aspects of qi to all the organs and to the muscles, tendons etc. In martial terms, the practitioner is able to harness all his power out to the point of contact. Chen Zhaopi likens this idea to an angry animal with its hair standing on end as it prepares to fight - *"nu fa chong guan怒发冲冠"*.

As blood is a fluid, its second important function is to moisten and lubricate the body. Chinese medical theory also suggests that blood plays a vital role in the development of lucid and stable thought processes. A blood deficiency may manifest through mood changes such as irritability, anxiety etc., which is not a good basis for martial efficiency. The close relationship between qi and blood is encapsulated in the saying, *"qi is the commander of blood, and blood is the mother of qi"* (Williams, 1996).

The tongue is believed to be the extremity of the flesh; the teeth the extremity of the bones; and the nails the extremity of the tendons. When the extremity of the flesh is amply supplied, the tongue is said to be strong enough to break the teeth; when the bones are filled with qi, they become dense and strong leading to the saying, *"the teeth can cut through metal"* (*duan jin* 断金); and when the tendons are saturated with qi, the fingers are said to be able to *"penetrate bones"*. Chen Zhaopi stressed the importance of realising the four extremities through sustained good quality practice.

Considered from a Western perspective these notions may seem abstruse and fanciful. However, Chen Zhaopi's theoretical framework is built upon a complex inter-related view of how the human organism functions most efficiently. Within traditional Chinese medicine two other critical components must be considered in interpreting his intended meaning accurately – *jing* 精 (essence) and *shen* 神 (spirit). According to Williams (1996) *jing* is responsible for the growth of bones, teeth and hair" and *"the strength of our jing determines our basic constitutional strength"*. Jing is also closely associated with the function of the kidneys. *"Kidney qi is the root of all the qi in the body, and if it is in any way deficient or weak this will lead to deficiency and weakness of the qi of the whole body"*.

Shen 神 is variously translated as "spirit" or "mind". But from this perspective is more than simply the mind that thinks, memorises and performs logical processes. Traditionally *shen* is considered within the context of its relationship with qi and *jing*. *Jing*, qi and *shen* 精, 气, 神 are referred to collectively in Chinese medicine as the "Three Treasures 三宝" and are held to be the essential components of life itself. *"Jing is the densest*

The Essence of Taijiquan 太極之粹

Chen Bing 20th Generation Chen Taijiquan descendent – when the Three Treasures are in harmony the individual will radiate with life: physically fit, mentally sharp and alert.

component and is responsible for the developmental processes of the body. Qi is the next stage and is responsible for the more immediate animate life of the body. Shen is the most refined level responsible for human consciousness. When the Three Treasures are in harmony the individual will radiate with life: physically fit, mentally sharp and alert" (Williams, 1996).

Paradoxically, during practice a Taijiquan player is advised not to think too much about the movement of qi in the body. Traditional teachers generally do not like to discuss qi with learners until they have attained some degree of proficiency. Although *yunqi* is a core component of Taijiquan, becoming fixated upon it is a sure way to impede progress. It is often said that if you concentrate upon the qi your spirit will be dull and lifeless. This theory is reflected in a verse from the Taiji Canon:

*"Lian li bu lian qi*练理不练气 (Train the principle not the qi)
*Lian qi ze zhi*练气则滞 (Training qi results in stagnation)
*Zhi ze bu ling*滞则不灵 (Stagnation results in a lack of agility)
*Lian li, li zhi er qi zhuang*练理，理直而气壮" (Train following the principle – the principle will be correct and the qi will be strong).

Closely following the Taijiquan principles during training provides the practitioner with a tangible starting point and an unambiguous idea of where their practice is going. Zhu Tiancai, one of Chen Zhaopi's most talented disciples, supports this practical approach. The training process involves a clear logical progression initially requiring the student to learn the correct structural alignment of the body. Through repetitive practice of *zhan zhuang* 站桩 (standing pole), *chansigong*缠丝功 (silk reeling exercises and the foundation form *Laojia Yilu* 老架一路 (Old Frame First Routine) the learner becomes familiar with the precise physical requirements of Chen style Taijiquan. Essential requirements include: relaxing and eradicating all tension from the body; storing the chest; relaxing the shoulders and allowing the elbows to sink down; and loosening the *kua* 胯(the point where the thighs meet the pelvis) at the same time as tucking in the lower back. *"In following these key points your qi will freely flow down to the legs and feet facilitating a strong foundation to build up qi throughout your whole body. You then* train partner drills and then martial applications and as a result intuitive responses will become effortless and not reliant on muscular strength."

Similarly, to the question whether one should focus on practicing Taijiquan movements or on qi manipulation? Chen Xiaowang answered as follows: *"If your movement is not correct, your qi will not flow… Every time you move – whether you are practicing the routines, push-hands or weapons – every movement, if it is not correct, the movement will be empty. As a result, your form would be purely physical. There will be no qi inside. This is a very important point"*. Chen Xiaowang also advises practitioners to let part of the mind be free during practice and to allow "being natural be the first principle 自然第一".

Understanding Chansijin

"To play Taijiquan one needs to understand chansijin 缠丝劲 (silk-reeling energy). Chansi is the method by which to move the zhong 中 (central) qi. If you don't understand this, you don't understand the boxing".

– Chen Family Record

It is said that an individual cannot claim to be practicing Taijiquan without understanding *chansijin*. Chen Zhaopi said, *"Playing Taijiquan is training neijin 内劲 (internal strength) and neijin is chansijin 缠丝劲"*. But how can we recognise *chansijin*? In essence silk reeling energy in Chen style Taijiquan training *"simply describes a stage where there is no flat surface, no straight lines, and the whole body becomes a circle from top to bottom"*. The *jin* 劲 (trained energy) in Taijiquan is executed from a circle and expressed in spirals and arcs. Moving in this circular manner ensures that the Taijiquan exponent's actions are unbroken and dynamic. Consequently, by eliminating any straight lines, level surfaces, kinks and breaks in movements and always seeking to make every position and action round an individual will be on the correct path (Source: Zhu Tiancai – *An Examination of Gongfu in Chenjiagou Taijiquan*).

An often-quoted verse from Taiji classics states, *"If you want to learn boxing well you must train until the circle is small"*. *Chansijin* is the method by which circular movement is established. With time and experience the process of training Taijiquan moves naturally from big circle to medium circle, from medium circle to small circle, and from small circle to no circle. Zhu Tiancai explained that *"no circle" does not mean the absence of circular movement; it simply means that the circle is not visible to an observer. However, there is always the intention of a circle. Learners sometimes think that circle means the parameter of the hands and feet and this is understandable…because the internal energy is not strong enough, a beginner needs to execute big movements. But when the internal energy becomes abundant then the big circle will become smaller"*.

Chansijin is derived from the study of *jingluo* 经络 – the network through which blood and qi continually circulates throughout the human body. Traditional Chinese medical theory holds that the channels and meridians that constitute the *jingluo* network originate from the internal organs, or *zhang fu*, and radiate out to the extremities of the body. Any disparity between the internal organs, the blood and the qi is believed to disturb the body's equilibrium and sooner or later result in illness. On the other hand, if all of these are co-ordinated and strong it can preserve health and increase an individual's lifespan.

The meridian network is made up of twelve regular channels corresponding to six yin organs – lung, heart, liver, kidney, spleen and the pericardium – and six yang organs – large intestine, small intestine, gall bladder, bladder, stomach and the triple burner *(san jiao* 三焦*)*. There are also eight "extraordinary channels" which are not directly linked to the organ network. The eight extraordinary channels consist of the: *renmai* 任脉 (conception vessel), *dumai* 督脉 (governing vessel), *chongmai* 冲脉 (penetrating vessel), *daimai* 带脉 (girdle vessel), *yinweimai* 阴维脉 (yin linking vessel), *yangweimai* 阳维脉 (yang linking vessel), *yinqiaomai* 阴蹻脉 (yin heel vessel) and *yangqiaomai* 阳蹻脉 (yang heel vessel). Of these, the

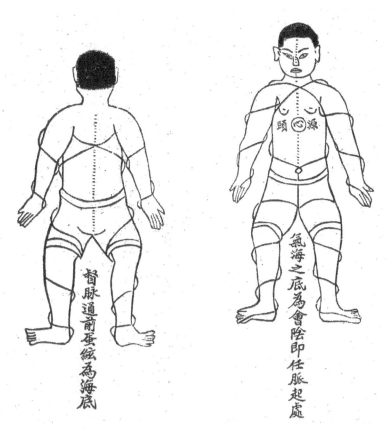

Front and back view of the chansijin route: Source Chen Xin's *Illustrated Explanation of Chen Family Taijiquan*.

renmai (down the front midline of the body) and *dumai* (running along the spine) are considered to be the most significant. The precise functions of the extraordinary channels include: acting as reservoirs of qi and blood for the twelve regular channels filling and emptying as required; circulating *jing* around the body because they have a strong connection with the kidneys; helping to circulate the defensive *weiqi* 卫气 over the trunk of the body thereby helping to maintain optimum health.

Of the benefit of *chansijin* Chen Zhenglei explains: *"Taijiquan's spiral silk-*

reeling movements direct and aid the circulation of qi and blood flow so that they flow smoother and stronger. In traditional Chinese medicine abundance of blood and qi keeps acute illness at bay, therefore lessening the likelihood of illness. This is why Taiji is seen as a health giving discipline". Chansijin originates from the kidneys, and should be present in every part of the body concerned with circulation. Chen Zhaopi writes, *"one is able to bring it to the hundred bones, the four extremities and through to the seven orifices. Prolonged practice enables your body to have boundless internal power, which is all absorbed and stored in your bones, circulating and flowing through your blood".*

"Internal qi is sourced from the dantian. Using the waist as the axis, the spiral movements combined with turning the waist and rotation of the spine lead to the kidney area being subtly stimulated. This enables qi to circulate freely throughout the body: through the renmai and dumai channels; exercising the daimai and chongmai and then reaching the four extremities, before returning to the dantian".

At a practical level, silk reeling exercises open up the body's joints, increasing one's flexibility. In training it requires the shoulders to be loose, elbows to be lowered, chest to be contained, waist folded, kua to be opened and knees to be bent and the waist to act as the hub of every movement. The joints are traditionally viewed as gateways for qi. Opening these gateways thus allows the unimpeded flow of qi required for the development of internal energy. A stiff joint represents a blockage obstructing the circulation of qi.

Silk reeling energy can be expressed through every aspect of a trained exponent's movement. It consists of "upward reeling, downward spiral, left-right, in-out, big-small, *shun-ni* 順逆 (natural-adverse) and *zheng-dao* 正倒 (direct-reverse), etc". At its core, *chansijin* provides a means by which to concentrate and circulate qi - bringing it to focus at one point and then turning it. Chen Zhaopi cautioned that when teaching Taijiquan it is not necessary to point out which part of the body is doing which reeling

The Essence of Taijiquan 太極之粹

19th Generation Chen Taijiquan adept Zhu Tiancai

method. This can actually be detrimental to the student, restricting the natural flow between movements necessary in Taijiquan thus compromising the underlying principle. It is sufficient to distinguish between *shun chan - ni chan* and *zheng chan – dao chan*. He gave a few examples from the Taiji form: "*Yun Shou* 云手 (Cloud Hands) is *zheng* 正 (direct) *chansijin* and *Dao Juan Hong* 倒卷宏 (Step Back and Whirl Arms) is *dao* 倒 (reverse) *chansijin*. In *Dan Bian* 单鞭 (Single Whip) the left side of the body is *zheng* and the right is *dao chansijin*". Zhu Tiancai concurs with this: "*Although Chen Family Taijiquan requires the practitioners to adhere to the principle of chansijin in every movement, it is not possible to expect a beginner to be able to do this. In fact he should not think about chansijin or qi circulation at all. At this stage it is sufficient to follow the instruction of a good teacher and practice diligently to standardise the external movements in order to prepare the path for internal movements*".

Chen Taijiquan's Unique Silk Reeling Movement

Chen Taijiquan's characteristic silk-reeling movement is built upon the rule of circular motion. Using the waist as the hub every movement must be round, each circle consisting of an equal measure of yin and yang or *shun chan* (natural reeling) and *ni chan* (reverse reeling). To take the spiralling of the hand as an example, when spiralling inwards the hand leads the elbow, the elbow leads the shoulder and the shoulder drives the waist. This is *shun chan* 顺缠 and corresponds to yin. When the hand rotates outwards, the waist drives the shoulder, the shoulder leads the elbow, and the elbow leads the hand. This is *ni chan* 逆缠 and corresponds to yang. Chen Xiaowang often uses the analogy of the turning on and off of an electric light bulb to illustrate this process. *Ni chan* is like the switching on of the electric current, power going out to the extremity. In this case the light bulb, in the previous example, the hand. *Shun chan* is the opposite. The electric current is switched off, the light is turned off and power stored in the battery or, in the case of the body, in the dantian.

Silk reeling energy must be present throughout the three sections of the body (upper limbs, torso and lower limbs). The upper limbs involve rotating the wrists and turning the arms; the torso involves rotating the waist and turning the back; and the lower limbs involve rotating the ankles and turning the legs. The three sections of the body will then combine to exhibit rootedness at the feet, control at the waist and manifestation in the hands. Fulfilling this principle indicates the synchronisation of the internal and external aspects of Taijiquan and sets the basic standard for the 'gongfu' of a practitioner. An old Chenjiagou saying is that: Everyone is equipped with Taiji, progress depends on whether one studies diligently.

Three Sections of the Body

"When you have reached a stage of success, then one expression of qi will saturate the whole body, so the whole body moves"

- Chen Zhaopi

The body is divided into three sections – upper, middle and lower - each with its own distinct requirements. The upper section is represented by the practitioner's head and is considered to be the commander of the rest of the body. Chen Zhaopi offers the following guidelines for the upper section: *"You must not incline your head. You must not shake the head or push your head upwards stiffly. The head is kept naturally upright, with the eyes looking level and forwards. When moving your hand, look at the nail of your middle finger. Lips are closed, tongue touching the upper palate in order to breathe naturally"*. Practicing Taijiquan without understanding the rules for the upper section leads to the whole body being dispersed with no clear focal point.

The middle section is comprised of the area from the throat down to the dantian. Of the middle section Chen Zhaopi instructed: *"Do not bend your waist or protrude your buttocks. Do not stick your stomach out or fill the chest. Relax the shoulders and sink the elbows. Store the chest and fold the waist. The spirit and qi should be calm"*. In combat terms, correct use of the waist is most vital. He likens the waist to the axis of a wheel, and qi to the wheel itself. The waist controls the whole body. If you do not understand waist power, the whole body will not be integrated.

The middle section can be further subdivided into three sections: the hand is the outer section, the elbow the middle section and the waist the root section. When executing a closing movement the hand leads the elbow, the elbow leads the shoulder and the shoulder leads the waist. In opening movements the opposite applies with the waist leading the shoulder, the shoulder leading the elbow and elbow leading the hand. This illustrates the movement principle of the outer section leading, the middle section following and the root section driving. This applies to both sides of the body, and enables energy to flow through in sequence.

The lower section is the area from the top of the thighs to the bottom of the feet. Failure to follow the requirements of the lower section will inevitably give rise to postural instability. Chen Zhaopi lists many strict requirements for the lower body, and cautions that weight distribution should be very precise at all times in order not to exhibit double weightedness. The heels should hold the floor with the *yongquan* 涌泉穴 acupoint (in the middle of the foot) kept empty; the kneecap should be held parallel to the heel and not allowed to be collapsed forward or pushed too far outwards; the *weizhong* acupoint 委中穴 at the back of the knee cannot be allowed to become weak; the foot should be turned in on the non-weight bearing leg, to express *chansijin* in the leg; the *fengmai* (飞脉穴)acupoint (situated in the inside thigh/kua) should be relaxed and insubstantial to enable the body to turn flexibly and freely; and the crotch (*dang* 裆) must be held in an open rounded position so that the body's strength can descend into the legs. The rules of the three sections should always apply: the coordination of the movements of the upper and lower limbs – hands with feet, elbows with knees and shoulders with hips.

In Taijiquan, *xiapan* 下盘 or lower body stability represents the foundation for all other skills and together with the correct lower body requirements enables the practitioner to display the nimble and agile footwork characteristic of Chen style Taijiquan. Chen Zhaopi illustrates the experience of *xiapan* stability through the idea of seeking lightness at the top and solidity at the bottom as expressed in the saying *"externally soft, internally strong"*. He emphasises the critical importance of understanding and applying the requirements of the lower section saying that: *"If you don't do it correctly, you will have no strength in the legs. It is like building the roof of a house on a crooked beam – it is impossible for it to stay and it will just collapse"*.

The Essence of Taijiquan 太極之粹

The body is divided into three sections – upper, middle and lower – each with its own distinct requirements.

The Yellow Emperor's Internal Canon: "The Dantian, three inches below the navel, is the gateway of yin and yang".

The Dantian – Gateway of Yin and Yang

Chen style Taijiquan practice constantly emphasises the importance of the *dantian*. The *dantian* is regarded as a main focal point for internal martial arts theory and breathing techniques as well as for traditional Chinese medicine and refers specifically to the physical center of gravity located in the lower abdomen three finger widths below and two finger widths behind the navel. The term *dantian* 丹田 (*dan-elixir; tian-field*) first appears in the great third century classic of Daoism alchemy and meditation, the *Huangting Waijing Jing* 黄庭外景经 (Canon of the Outer Radiance of the Yellow Court), which stated that, *"through respiration, original qi enters the dantian. The dantian, three inches below the navel, is the gateway of yin and yang"*.

The one overriding principle underpinning the practice of Taijiquan often referred to by the teachers can be encapsulated in the phrase *"when the dantian moves, the whole body moves".* This means that no part of the body moves independently from the rest of the body – when any one part of the body is in motion, the entire body moves, and the movement is driven by the dantian. From the centre, *jin* 劲 is transmitted to each section of the body in a wavelike action. When an individual's movement is correctly initiated from the dantian, qi circulates in an uninterrupted way and the centre is maintained at all times. Skilled exponents often refer to a distinct feeling of a sphere in the abdomen that is turning as they practice Taijiquan.

While the dantian itself has little strength, it is helpful to think of it as the co-ordinating point or central hub of one's movement. To apply force, the movement of the dantian must be synchronised with the rest of the body. The force generated initiates from the dantian and co-ordinates with the rest of the body, gaining force along the way. Chen Xiaowang explains,

"You coordinate the rest of the body with the source, the dantian. When the dantian starts to move every part of the body move simultaneously, all connected to each other. You connect the muscles of the legs and the back to follow it. The body then pushes the hands, which express the force. It is a three-dimensional movement, utilising the whole body. The dantian, hip, knee and leg all synchronise setting off the spiralling motion throughout the body. The dantian area by itself does not have much force. But when it is coordinated with the rest of the body, it can coordinate a lot of power. When you initiate movement from the dantian area, the energy from the dantian will communicate with the rest of the body. Then together, the energy becomes a strong force."

The natural extension of this highly focused spiral movement is the capacity to exhibit great explosive power. *"The body moves as a co-ordinated whole because of dantian movement. While issuing power (fali* 发力*), dantian turns and the whole body power is focused on one point. In this way the power issued can penetrate the bones of an opponent"* (Feng Zhiqiang 冯志强).

By focusing one's consciousness on the dantian region the Taijiquan practitioner can derive a number of benefits: it serves to lower the body's centre of gravity, thus increasing the stability and balance of the lower plane (*xiapan* 下盘); when combined with Taijiquan's spiral movement, it facilitates the gentle massage of the internal organs improving the function and health of those organs; focusing the intention on this area during practice helps the practitioner to quieten their mind of external distractions; alongside Taijiquan's correct postural framework it encourages deep abdominal breathing or *"dantian breathing"*, which serves to increase an individual's lung capacity.

The dantian stores qi like an energy reservoir, and also drives qi throughout the body, like a pump. However, qi on its own is of little functional use. A common saying when referring to internal martial arts such as Taijiquan is that one should employ internal strength rather than muscular power. This seems to be borne out by the subtly harmonised movements of skilled exponents who make it appear as if no muscular effort is involved. This is not quite true. What is actually required is the most efficient co-ordination of the internal and external aspects of the body. Chen Xiaowang explains: *"Qi by itself is soft and weak. The dantian stores qi and "communicates" it throughout the body to the muscles and bones. When qi is generated it is directed throughout the body by the jingluo*经络 *(network of channels and meridians). It is essential that one understand the connections between dantian and qi, qi and muscle, and muscle and bone. The key communication is that involving the dantian and the muscles of the body – this is the essence of Chen Taijiquan".*

Dantian rotation exercise

In Taijiquan training the dantian is strengthened by standing postures and through correct movement and alignment. In Chenjiagou practitioners traditionally train a specific "dantian rotation" exercise, which enables the learner to focus on the dantian area and begin to understand its rotational movements.

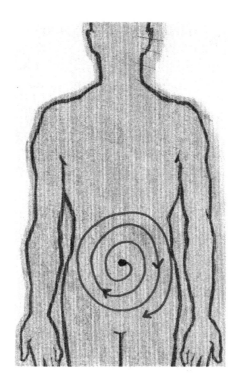

Place the hands over the dantian so that the *laogong* 劳功 points of the left and right hands line up with the dantian. For men, the left hand is held against the body covered by the right and 36 circles are made, going up the left side of the body and down the right side. For women the right hand is held against the body covered by the left and they are turned in the opposite direction.

With each successive rotation the circles grow larger until, after 36 rotations, when the hands are changed (i.e. for men the right hand is placed against the body covered by the left, vice versa for women) and the direction is reversed. This time 24 consecutively smaller circles are made returning to the dantian.

The exercise serves to prevent stagnation by dispersing qi that may be concentrated in the dantian after practicing standing for a period of time, returning the energy throughout the body.

Breathing in Taijiquan

> *"A true person's breath goes down to his heels"*
>
> - Zhuang Zi

From the moment of birth, an individual breathes continuously throughout the duration of their lifetime. This is a completely natural process affecting every part of the body from the muscles right down to the cellular level. The Chinese word "*shi*", 嘘 as well as denoting breath, has been used to mean "to refresh", "to recuperate" and sometimes is associated with the idea of growth. In terms of bodily vigour, the importance of the breath has been closely chronicled in Chinese literature. Mencius 孟子 (372– 289 BCE) spoke of the constant process of "growth and recuperation" in trees and in men "day and night", and we refer to the expelling of breath in respiration as *shi*. An old Chinese saying state: *"A person is born and dies with one breath"*; an individual is born with one clear breath that is then circulated throughout life, continually being exhaled and inhaled like the alternation of the sun and the moon, or like the ebb and flow of the tide. *"When a person falls ill, the breath becomes stagnant, and becomes less clear. When a person dies, it is as if they are blocked with mucous – the death rattle is not clear air"*.

Many practitioners spend a great deal of time debating how to breathe most efficiently when practicing Taijiquan. And many texts have been written about the correct method of breathing in Taijiquan. It is helpful to reveal some of the thoughts of past and present teachers of Chen Family Taijiquan in order to gain insight into this subject.

18th generation Chen family master Chen Zhaopi 陈照丕 suggested that in the beginning it is not helpful to think too much about breathing during your training: *"In the early stages of training there are many more pressing "problems" to deal with. The form must be practiced until the sequence is accurate and eloquent and the requirements for the hands, eyes, body, method and footwork are proficient".* *"When you are playing Taiji, you should not ask which posture is accompanied by exhaling (hu呼) and which posture is inhaling (xi吸) because this is not natural. This means that one is using the throat to breath…this type of breathing is not only unhealthy, but it can be harmful".*

Chen Xiaowang 陈小旺, the present standard-bearer, often tells students to breath naturally. He explains that an individual's breathing naturally regulates in line with their actions. For example, if a person starts to run, he does not need to command his breathing to speed up. The breathing will naturally adjust according to the body's need. As postures become more accurate and the Taijiquan's principle is followed, the breathing will adjust accordingly. In practice, there is little benefit to be gained from focusing upon breathing until one is completely familiar with the form and has reached a stage where, through a process of constant correction, every posture is fixed and will not deviate no matter which aspect of Taijiquan is being trained – weapons, push hands etc – then it is time to consider the important factor of breathing.

The Daoist texts call for practitioners to adhere to the adage *"xu zai xin shi zai fu虚在心, 实在腹"* or "insubstantial in the heart (chest) and substantial in the abdomen (the body's centre)". In order for the centre to be stable it involves training qi so that it accumulates in the lower abdomen.

The Taijiquan classic states: *"Able to breath, one will be agile and alive."* The skilled practice of Chen Taijiquan requires the use of deep abdominal breathing to bring qi to the dantian. Chen Zhaopi stated that dantian qi must be used when practicing Taijiquan. He explained that dantian qi is a natural form of qi starting even before birth: The foetus follows its mother's breath in the womb before birth. A person only starts to breathe on his own when the umbilical cord is cut. As an individual starts to breath independently, the umbilical cord contracts into the body and settles just under the navel. The qi that comes out from this opening is said to be dantian qi. *"This is in accordance with the Chinese belief that, when you breathe, as the* navel goes up and down we are continuing to breath qi in through that small orifice. As long as we can maintain this type of breathing we should be able to supply heat to the body and fluid to the internal organs". If the qi from this orifice is stagnant or slow, the person becomes ill. Chen Zhaopi believed that practicing Taijiquan was one means by which this qi could be encouraged to flow strongly, preventing stagnation and illness. He supported this with an old saying that while the: *"doctor treats your illness, Taiji treats your constitution"*.

Renowned Chen Style master Zhu Tiancai said: *"Abdominal breathing utilises the art of tuna*吐纳*, which is reverse breathing. Chen style Taijiquan training maintains a strong abdomen and wide chest (capacity) by bringing the tension of the chest down to the abdominal area so that the chest feels comfortable and wide. The abdominal region is relaxed but at the same time it is "chongshi*充实*" (full but not hard or tense, rather like when a balloon is filled with air)"*. This serves to increase the lung capacity letting in more air so that the exchange of gases is at its optimal level. Abdominal breathing also helps to enhance mental alertness, massages the internal organs, aids the circulation of qi and blood and regulates the breath so that breathing naturally co-ordinates with movements to realise the state of *"heart and sprit enters stillness*心神入静*"* and *"shape and spirit harmonises into one*形神合一*"*.

Once the concept of breathing and movement co-ordination is understood then, with further practice, movement and breathing will naturally become synchronised and in unison. The external shape and the internal energy harmonise as one or as the classics state literally *"become one entity"*. The abdominal region is full, the upper body is light and agile and the lower limbs are firm and stable.

Chen Zhaopi gives a general guideline for Taijiquan's "natural" breathing: *"movement is exhale, stillness is inhale; shun chan*顺缠 *(natural reeling) is exhale, ni chan*逆缠 *(reverse reeling) is inhale; qi going back to the dantian is storing (therefore it*

The abdominal region is relaxed but at the same time it is "chongshi" (full but not hard or tense – like a balloon filled with air).

is to inhale), qi going out of the dantian is action (therefore it is exhale)". Breathing in this manner, allows one to eliminate 'stale qi' (manifested by stiff musculature and awkwardness in movements) while at the same time accumulate clear qi (manifested by smooth unimpeded movements).

Tian Jingmiao 田京苗, an indoor disciple of Lei Muni 雷慕尼, explains that the basic breathing of Taijiquan uses the nose. There should be a "little breath" when turning the body and in between movements, and particularly in fajin 发劲 movements. A "little breath" means taking short breaths in between that the quality of relaxation and slight pause. This "little breath" directs the mind to calmness and the body to loosen. Inhalation and exhalation are converted alternately.

Considered within the context of combat technique the breathing method is particularly important. The successful execution of the combat techniques of Chen style Taijiquan requires the co-ordination of breathing in order for the whole body to work as one integrated unit. *"One inhalation one exhalation is equivalent to one hard and one soft, one substantial and one insubstantial, one drawing in and one going out, one storing and one releasing. The changes in breathing (tempo) are what cause the unifying of the two. The changes of breathing are done in a blink during actual combat and are made possible by the alternation of inhalation and exhalation. These rapid changes are what make the combat techniques of Chen Taijiquan possible".* (Zhu Tiancai, 1994).

What Attitude is Required to be Successful?
Training Culture

"Practice a thousand and ten thousand times, the skill you seek will naturally grow 千回万遍多多演，功到熟时巧自生*"*

- old martial arts saying

The Essence of Taijiquan 太極之粹

"Practice a thousand times, movements will be natural".

Chen Zhaopi is credited with revival of Taijiquan in its birthplace Chenjiagou and is the single most important influence in the Chen Family Taijiquan taught today. Whether or not a Taijiquan practitioner reaches a significant level of ability, he stated, depends ultimately on his/her attitude towards training. That once a person makes a decision to learn Taijiquan, he/she should be unwavering in the determination to grasp the entirety of the art.

Practice must be regarded as an essential part of one's life and the serious practitioner should practice every day; without exception and until it has become an unbreakable habit. *"Winter or summer, in wind or snow, there should be no interruption. In time the heart will accept and the spirit will understand, and the wonderment of the fist will be realised".*

This 'slow burn' approach calling for consistent daily training over a long period of time is reflected in the traditional saying: *"If you cast out the (fishing) net for three days and then dry it for two days you will be wasting your effort and will not reap any benefit 三天打鱼两天晒网, 徒劳无益"*. All accomplished master concur with this sentiment. For instance, Tian Jingmiao says that her morning Taijiquan practice is as essential as eating breakfast.

There are many accomplished practitioners throughout the generations of the Chen Family. Their accomplishment was a natural consequence of "treating ten years like one day" (*shi nian ru yi ri* 十年如一日). The results are a direct consequence of conscientious study combined with diligent training over a lifetime. Whatever stage of practice an individual is at, this level of commitment inevitably brings success. Regardless of starting points or levels of fitness: *"as long as they make it a long-term project, they will achieve. If you practice a thousand and ten thousand times, the skill you seek will naturally grow—taiji becomes instinctive and a part of you"*. In an article written in 1993 Chen Kesen 陈克森 recalled the dedication and constancy with which his father Chen Zhaopi approached his training: "My father practiced Taijiquan exceptionally hard when he was young, doing thirty sets a day regardless of weather conditions; every day without letting up".

Chen Zhaopi, however, cautioned students not to practice blindly. Training hard without thinking about the subtleties of Taijiquan, or just contemplating the finer points without training hard both lead to a *"failure to grasp the entirety of Taijiquan"*. In an article entitled *Scientific Principles and Methods of Chen style Taijiquan*, Hong Jun Sheng 洪筠生 remembers the primary importance his teacher, the legendary Chen Fake 陈发科, placed upon the necessity of practice being based upon an understanding of Taijiquan's underlying principles. Chen Fake reiterates to his students that there are three stages to achieving success in practice: *"The first stage is learning the basic movements correctly according to the rules; the second stage is becoming proficient in practicing the taolu 套路 (set of movements) according to the rules; the third stage is thorough familiarity with the rules and to meticulously seek out and to understand clearly why there are these rules"*.

The Essence of Taijiquan 太極之粹

The current Chen family gatekeeper Chen Xiaowang has divided progress, from the first movement until completion and success, into five distinct levels. At each level he sets objective targets for practitioners to gauge their own standard and progress – the fifth level representing the ultimate where one has successfully reached the highest level: *"From the beginning level through to the fifth level, each level has its requirements in order to reach the necessary standard. Taijiquan practitioners must clearly understand the level that they are at, know what level of gongfu they possess and what they need to do in order to progress to the next step. Learning Taijiquan is like learning in school. It must be done in the correct order, advancing gradually, level by level. If one goes against this order, like one in a primary school trying to understand the lessons of a university.*

As well as following the appropriate route of progress one must not be in a hurry for success. Impatience will impede progress and can lead to a loss of confidence. "A person needs to have an accurate and wholesome understanding of his level and stage of learning and then find the appropriate intensity and method of training that he can endure. This way it enables step-by-step progression to the final goal". (Chen Xiaowang – Zhonghua Wushu 中华武术杂志 magazine).

Often individuals, having seen the high levels of skill of Taijiquan masters or read/heard of the seemingly superhuman exploits of past masters, believe that there must be some special secrets handed down only to family members. Chen Bing陈炳, a twentieth generation of the Chen Family in Chenjiagou, dismissed this idea of exclusive transmission and knowledge. He said that the one real advantage of being a family member is the constant access to high-level teaching. This aside, any achievement is down to the hard work put in by an individual. Chen Zhaopi ridiculed the idea of special secrets as "completely unfounded". *"Besides having the direction of a good teacher, the main criterion is whether the person himself is willing to put in the hard work".*

Taijiquan requires long-term commitment. Many practitioners abandon it when they hit an obstacle. In an interview published in China's Zhonghua Wushu magazine 中华武术杂志, Chen Xiaowang quoted the adage: *"There are tens of thousands (people) learning quan拳, but those who have truly learned are in ones and tens".* He qualifies: *"Perhaps this saying is exaggerated, but it is true that a larger number of people who took up the art abandon it midway. The main reason is not being able to persevere, or due to a loss of confidence. There is no special remedy to overcome this, simply an unswerving mentality".*

Chen Xiaoxing陈小星, the leading Taijiquan teacher in Chenjiagou today, does not concur with the reasons people put forward for not being able to train. He was particularly dismissive of the common assertion that the modern pace of life makes it more difficult to find enough time to train to the extent that practitioners did in the past. *"Unfortunately this is the route you have to take, there are no two ways about it. People think that past teachers have a lot more time to practice. Work nowadays is actually a lot easier. People usually have a set time of maybe eight hours a day. When we did farm work in the past we didn't have machineries. Even when machines began to be used to ease physical labour we could not afford to buy them. Work was very hard and not limited to a few hours a day".*

Chen Bing: There are no secrets "any achievement is down to the hard work put in by an individual".

He is uncompromising in his opinion that if one is genuine about acquiring a superior level of Taiji skill, it has to involve self-discipline and organisation. For the average employee working an eight hour day, he suggests it should not be insurmountable to find two hours a day for taiji practice: *"You can comfortably manage ten repetitions of the form in two hours. Do this every day and in 365 days, imagine how many repetitions you will have done. It is all a matter of determination and perseverance - if you really want it".*

In a recent keynote address at a symposium in America, Ma Hailong, the son of the famous Wu Style exponent Ma Yueliang said of the quality of practice in his parents: *"They taught martial art as a career. They spent a long, long time every day practicing martial arts. Today people cannot put so much effort into their practice. It is almost impossible"* (T'ai Chi Magazine, 2009).

Chen Xiaoxing concluded that it is consistency that will eventually bring results. *"Repetitive practice of the form leads to complete familiarity with the movements. Over the course of time co-ordination and flexibility are naturally attained throughout every move contained within a form. What you must aim for is to be able to perform every movement in a fluid and unpredictable manner, shifting without warning from slow to fast, from soft to hard, and from light to heavy."*

Sixteenth generation practitioner Chen Xin陈鑫 advised: *"if you don't understand the principle consult a good teacher; if you don't understand the route, visit a sincere friend".* Two generations later, Chen Zhaopi expanded on this suggestion, that once an individual had understood the principle and was clear about the route then they should *"add to their daily toil, keep practicing, press forward and don't regress. In time it will inevitably come to you".* A saying handed down in Chenjiagou is *"quan da yi qian bian bu da zhi cuan* 拳打一千遍，不打自传*"* or *"practice quan (boxing) a thousand times, the skill will transmit itself".*

Chen Xiaoxing: "consistency brings results"

The Three Stages of Progression

1. Opening the Joints

Chen Zhaopi identified three distinct stages that all Taijiquan practitioners must go through. The first phase involves training the body externally, concentrating upon the extremities. During this period, with much repetitive practice, one acquires familiarity of the form. Deficient in internal energy, the learner manifests a state of being *"externally hard and internally empty"*.

During this stage of progression, the learner trains a very external form of *jin* 劲 (power) that is very different from that of an accomplished player. Movements tend to be unrestrained and forceful. He gave the following examples to illustrate this: during *Yang Shou Hong Quan* 掩手宏拳 (Hidden Thrust Punch), the fist is thrown out forcefully; in *Bai Jiao* 摆脚 (Cross Kick) the kick is executed too vigorous; performing *Jin Ji Du Li* 金鸡独立 (Golden Rooster Stands on One Leg) or *Er Ti Jiao* 二踢脚 (Double Raise Foot) the upward lift is abrupt; and postures such as *Jin Gang Dao Dui* 金刚捣碓 (Buddha's Warrior Attendant Pounds Mortar) or *Die Cha* 跌岔 (Drop Split) are characterised by the student dropping down violently.

Though seeming to contradict the ultimate goal of fluid, controlled and internally driven movements, this stage is however necessary. Chen Zhaopi says, *"if first you don't train this kind of brute jin, the body's joints will not be opened up and flexible. As a result, the neijin (internal energy) cannot be stimulated"*.

This primary stage is a process by which the aim is to train the hand techniques *zhua na shuai da* 抓拿摔打 (grab, seize, throw and hit). Although movements may be overly expansive and uncoordinated, it is impossible for a person to be able to execute the more complex and intricate aspects straightaway. Logically, if the student cannot effectively control their limbs, how can they expect to control the many subtle facets of the body? To gain this control, when training one must meticulously consider and revise every movement contained within the form: *"every posture, every technique, every twist and turn, every corner must be studied carefully – if you don't study carefully, then the whole body will not move smoothly"*.

The first stage can be expected to take about five years in order to lay down a good foundation. The five years entail rigorous daily training under the guidance of a knowledgeable teacher. The first stage is deemed successful when movements become pliant, fluid and lively. For example:

Stamping the foot in *Jing Gang Dao Dui* 金刚捣碓 should sound like thunder.

Punching out during *Yang Shou Hong Quan* 掩手宏拳 should make a noise like the wind.

Leaping up to execute *Er Ti Jiao* 二踢脚, the kick should be able to reach seven or eight foot into the air.

Performing *Die Cha* 跌岔 both legs must get down to the ground and then leap up again without using the hands for assistance.

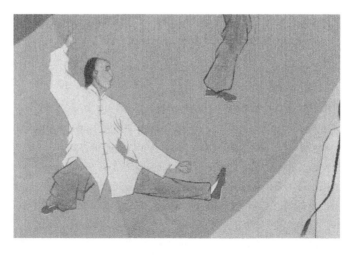

Die Cha: Performing this posture "both legs must get down to the ground and then leap up again without using the hands for assistance".

Dashing forwards during *Yu Nu Chuan Suo*玉女穿梭 (Jade Girl Works at Shuttles) should be completed *'with the speed of a typhoon'*.

2. Understanding Internal Energy - Dong Jin 懂劲

On reaching the second stage, a practitioner is ready to begin the long journey towards understanding *neijin* (internal energy): *"Qi moves the external shape of the body; If qi doesn't move, the shape remains still; When qi moves, the shape follows; External shape and internal qi are unified; Light at the top, solid at the bottom; Soft on the outside, strong on the inside"*.

Chen Zhaopi suggests a careful study of the following thirteen entities that are qualities that are manifested when the internal energy is unified: *zhan* 沾 (stick), *you* 游 (flow), *lian* 连 (connect), *sui* 随 (follow), *teng* 腾 (leap), *shan* 闪 (dodge), *zhe* 折 (fold), *kong* 空 (empty), *peng* 掤 (ward off), *lu* 捋 (divert), *ji* 挤 (squeeze), *an* 按 (press), and *huo* 活 (lively). This study forms the essence of Taijiquan and is the basis of the second phase.

Zhan 沾 (stick): enables the whole form to "stick or hold together, and all aspects of movements be unified and not dispersed".

You 游 (flow): "movements should flow with no breaks or gaps". Any feeling of awkwardness and any constricted movement point to a lack of flow. To ensure that one possesses the correct quality of flow, the Taijiquan practitioner must *'yong yi bu yong li*用意不用力*'* *(conscious use of intention rather than strength)* throughout practice. At the end of each movement, the intention should not stop even if the movement have come to a pause.

Jin Ji Du Li – an example of *teng jin*

Lian 连 (connect): from start to finish each movement is connected to the next. In push hands, *lian* denotes an energy that links or connects with the partner's energy.

Sui 随 (follow): "the whole body follows, circulating and spiralling at will". Chen Zhaopi admonished practitioners not to *"let an opponent use you like a walking stick"*. In other words, by carefully following rather than resisting an opponent's action, it gives no opportunity for him to apply his strength against you. To follow effectively it is important that you are able to change naturally and spontaneously as the opportunity arises. Hesitating when a chance presents itself, or trying to pre-empt an opponent's movement, signify a failure to follow.

Teng 腾 (leap): a forceful jump or a sudden abrupt rising movement is said to be *teng*. Examples in the handform include Double Raise Leg *Er Ti Jiao* 二踢脚 or *Jin Ji Du Li* 金鸡独立 Golden Rooster Stands on One Leg.

Shan 闪 (dodge): is a method of avoiding or dodging an opponent's attack to one's upper body. This is performed with great speed and suddenness to create a space between oneself and an attacker. *Shan* is characterised by movements initiated from a high to a low position and, as well as great swiftness, requires critical timing to be effective. Examples in the handform include *Shan Tong Bei* 闪通背 (Flash through the Back) and *Pie Shen Quan* 撇身拳 (Flinging Body).

Zhe 折 (fold/turn over): a frequently utilised tactic by experienced Taijiquan exponents, the idea of *zhe* is often misapplied by students as it requires precise timing so as not to commit the error of using force against force. Chen Zhaopi gave this example: In pushing hands, as an opponent is led into emptiness, resulting in over-extension, he would draw back in an effort to re-stabilise his position; at that precise moment follow the returning movement of the opponent by vigorously adding force to it. He listed the postures *Man Toh Sao Xue* 满头扫雪 and *Bai Ma Wo Cao* 白马卧槽 as instances where jin is returned.

Lan Zha Yi Posture

The Essence of Taijiquan 太極之粹

Kong 空 (empty): refers to the idea of "leading an opponent into void and then utilising this empty space to attack". This type of change is employed frequently throughout the form, for example in *Lan Zha Yi* 懒扎衣 (Lazily Tying Coat) - as the right foot steps out to enter an opponent's space, the right arm draws back to lead them into an over-extended and vulnerable position.

Peng 掤 (ward off): often cited as the most important energy within the realm of Taijiquan. *Peng jin* should be present throughout every movement and *"all eight directions should have peng jin"*. Chen Zhaopi asks the question, *"why is it when someone steps on top of a ball they feel as if they want to fall off"*? His answer points to the nature of Taijiquan itself: *"It's because there are no flat surfaces on a ball, so the ball rolls the person off. So in boxing, the jin has to be trained to become a complete sphere with no flat surface, so people roll off into emptiness"*.

Lu 捋 (divert): is often mistakenly practiced as a pulling type of *jin*, however, it would be more accurate to describe it as a form of leading or drawing energy. The function of *lu* is to redirect an opponent's energy diagonally from front to back, and can be applied in an upward or downward direction. Examples of *lu* in the handform include the transition from *Lan Zha Yi* 懒扎衣 (Lazily Tying Coat) to *Liu Feng Si Bi* 六封四闭 (Six Sealing and Four Closing) and *Ye Ma Fen Zong* 野马分鬃 (Parting the Wild Horse's Mane).

Ji 挤 (squeeze): Chen Zhaopi likened *ji* to the Taijiquan technique *kao* (lean/bump). However, whereas *kao* is applied explosively, *ji* is used to crowd or squeeze into an opponent's centre as they are withdrawing. In his words: *"Ji also contains kao* 靠 *(bump) method. So, it can be separated into the zuo xiong kao and you xiong kao* 左右胸靠 *(left and right bumps with chest), yin men kao* 迎门靠 *(open and bump), shi zi kao* 十字靠 *(crossover bump) and bei zhe kao (bump with back)* 背折靠.

An 按 (press): requires the practitioner to push their opponent with both hands. Examples of *an* in the handform include the movements *Shuang Tui Shou* 双推手 (Two Hands Push Forwards) and *Bao Tou Tui Shan* (Cover Head Push Mountain) 抱头推山.

Huo 活 (lively): the previous twelve characteristics must be executed with flexibility and liveliness. Chen Zhaopi explained: *"if the technique is lifeless it is not usable, you have to keep it alive. This means that when you are pushing hands with somebody you have to change according to the situation"*. Taijiquan is built upon the qualities of agility and responsiveness.

The second phase of the training process concentrates primarily upon the middle section of the body. *"In practical usage, you would be using your shoulder, elbow, kua and knee. Train the middle section to attack your opponent"*. Besides the different aspects being trained, Chen Zhaopi suggested that there is a distinct difference in how one should approach the first two stages of progression. As mentioned, the first stage calls upon the learner to carefully examine how to let *jin* reach the extremities, i.e. to the hands and feet. During the second stage, analysing too much can actually be detrimental to one's progress. For practitioners working through this phase, he offers the following words of advice: *"Don't think about it too much, or you will commit the error of moving the part that you are thinking of without it being supported by the rest of the body...don't scrutinise too much... don't hesitate...let the movement be natural"*. This stage can be completed successfully if one is prepared to train continually for an extended period. Chen Zhaopi suggested that if an individual did not commit to a minimum of ten years, it is unlikely that they would *"reach the standard of what is required in the thirteen postures"*.

In order to gauge whether one has successfully navigated the second phase, he laid down the following six sensations that one should feel:

- The *dantian* 丹田 area feels sunken.

- The *panguang* 膀胱 (area around the urinary bladder) has a distinct feeling of warmth.

- The heels feel heavy.

- There is a sensation of the head being suspended from above.

- The muscles and flesh feels pumped up and expansive.

- The fingers have a sensation of numbness and tingling.

By the time the second phase is reached a practitioner can effectively combine the external shape (*waixing* 外形) and internal qi. At this stage, it can be said that the student has understood the principles of Taijiquan: its body mechanics, movement principles, postural requirements etc. However, *"to have learned the correct training method does not mean that one has accomplished skill 学人规矩不能学人巧"*. On reaching this level, a practitioner should be able to train in the absence of a teacher and not deviate from the right path. This, though, is simply one more step on the road to mastery. Skill is only achieved through repeated training. Once you have learned the method from the teacher, then you have to practice diligently and consistently until total familiarity makes it become a part of you. By training in this manner, the practitioner can gradually move into the third phase.

3. Executing Continuous Movements in One Breath

The third level of *gongfu* concerns being "perfectly rounded". At this stage a practitioner should manifest the perfect blend of alternating hard and soft movements and combination and coordination of large and small circles.

Chen Zhaopi used sixteen Chinese words to describe the characteristics of the third stage, broken down into four-character descriptions *"缓慢柔活，平稳舒展，连绵贯穿，呼吸自然"* as follows:

***Huan Man Rou Huo* 缓慢柔活** –relaxed, slow, soft and pliant. A Taijiquan exponent must train *"to a stage where there is a co-ordination of softness (rou柔) and hardness (gang刚)"* and also to *"train until the circle is so small that it is not discernible from the outside"*. While not visible from the outside, there should always be the presence of circularity throughout the entire body, described by Chen Zhaopi as: *"being so small that they (the circles) are inside your five organs and hundred bones"*.

The slower a person trains, the faster he would be able to emit power when required. Chen Taiji theorists often write that hardness and speed arises from the prolonged accumulation of softness and slowness: *"Still as a mountain and swift like lightning. Like a crash of thunder – it is so sudden that one has no time to cover the ears"*.

The storing and releasing of *jin*劲 is compared with drawing a bow and firing an arrow. The bowstring is pulled back gradually until it is rounded and energy is stored in the limbs of the bow, which is then transformed into rapid motion when the string is released, transferring great force to the arrow. The four-word formula *huan man rou huo* can be understood exactly as this example, *"storing jin in the body is like drawing the bow, releasing jin through the extremities is like the firing of an arrow"*.

***Ping Wen Shu Zhan*平稳舒展** – where movements are *"balanced, steady, smooth and unrestricted"*. When moving a practitioner's posture should be *"dafang*大方*"* meaning poised and unaffected. Movements therefore are natural *(ziran*自然*)*, uninhibited and comfortable. Each posture should appear instinctive and unplanned. Chen Zhaopi uses the expression *"shen hui*神会*"* to describe movements that are so instinctive you don't have to think about them, they seem to come out spontaneously. *Shenhui* refers to a state where a practitioner is wholly engaged in his activity, as if it is part of the soul. The body's energies follow the mind's intentions. Within the boxing there is limitless potential and when the *gongfu* 功夫 *(skill)* is trained it can be summoned at will.

Storing and releasing jin is compared with drawing a bow and firing an arrow.

***Lian Mian Guan Chuan*连绵贯穿** – movements are linked, unbroken and running through. *Chansijin*缠丝劲 (silk reeling energy) is present in all movements, which must be performed in an unbroken flow: *"Use the intention (yi*意*) and not strength (li*力*). When yi stops, jin does not break. Form movements should be like a string of pearls all linked together"*.

***Hu Xi Zi Ran*呼吸自然** – breathing is natural. Breathing is not forced and is allowed to naturally regulate itself in coordination with movements.

Chen Xiaowang often explains that our breathing naturally changes its pattern when we change from walking to running. In the same way the breathing pattern adjusts as a Taijiquan practitioner's postures and movements alter and become closer to the standards laid down. *"Even after many repetitions of the form, breathing must remain comfortable and not laboured. The face does not change colour and speech is normal"*.

The third level of *gongfu* is complete when an individual has realised the properties of these sixteen Chinese characters and all techniques are incorporated inside the body ready to be brought out at will. Skills become more internalised so they become less obvious to the untrained eye. Like a Chinese herbal soup, through prolonged brewing all the goodness of the herbs are contained within the decoction. However, it is impossible to identify the individual ingredients. At this stage, *"whether it is hitting or throwing, whether it is rising or dropping, whether it is shoulder or elbow strikes etc., all the techniques are contained within"*. A superior strength is hidden within, and any part of the body can be used for attack.

The third stage is the stage where the "small circle becomes no circle". At this advanced level the outer shape offers no clue as to the changes taking place within the body. All the movement principles and body requirements have been realised, but improvement is still possible with continuous practice. Zhu Tiancai wrote: *"The path will not deviate but the quality of gongfu can still be improved. For example, the quality of the alternation of hard and soft is not uniform between practitioners. Each day's practice brings a new level of realisation and a new level of gongfu"*.

With completion of the third stage, Chen Zhaopi pointed to a number of physical sensations one would experience, including a feeling concentrated heat in the kidney and bladder areas *panguang*膀胱. The internal organs are well diffused, like plants that have been well watered and are moist and lubricated on the inside.

While verbal instructions can point an individual in the right direction, it is often impossible to thoroughly vocalise the complexities of Taijiquan. Each stage has to be worked through systematically, each success opening the door to the next stage, bringing a new level of understanding to the individual. Chen Xin concurs: *"All that idle talk does is to create a tide of black ink; putting it into practice is the real thing".*

Today, as language and writing becomes more explicit teaching tools, many people place greater importance on intellectual understanding over physical realisation. Speaking to the leading teachers from Chenjiagou it is clear that they did not engage in much verbal exchanges with their teachers. The traditional teachers consider that 'knowledge' results from 'doing'. One learns from one's practice and the constant observation of a teacher's form. Then from studying the form to studying the spirit, thus moving from the outward appearance to the inner content. This is *'wuxing悟性'*, or intuitive understanding.

Chen Zhenglei, in *Chenjiagou Chen Style Taijiquan* (1998) suggests that students should not look too far ahead from their current stage of development. The beginning students will naturally reach the first stage, i.e. familiarity with the form, if they adopt the traditional approach. Progress inevitably follows if one practices the First Frame routine up to repeatedly and consistently, paying attention to basic body mechanics, and striving to perform every movement in a soft, natural and balanced manner: *"In the beginning of your practice of Taijiquan, with respect to body mechanics, you are only required to keep your head naturally upright, stand straight, and don't lean over too far in any direction…as for those errors that unavoidably crop up, like raising your shoulders, sticking out your elbows, filling your chest with unrestrained qi, panting when you breathe etc. – it is not advisable to examine these phenomena too deeply".*

Chen Zhaopi concluded that even the most serious practitioners never totally master every aspect of Taijiquan: *"The gongfu is without boundary; even with a lifetime of training one does not completely get its complexity. If you train one level, you understand one level of complexity and thus it goes…"*

CHAPTER THREE

TAIJIQUAN AS A COMBAT ART

Chen Zhoukui: "I teach quan in order to teach combat"

Taijiquan as a Combat Art

For generations, Chen Taijiquan has been successfully used to develop the physical and mental attributes required for combat. However, Taijiquan remains something of an enigma. To the untrained eye, the slow routine of the system is not obviously martial. Consequently misunderstandings and misinterpretations abound. Perceptions of the true character of the art are often erroneous, with many viewing it as an exercise suitable only for the old and infirmed. The exercise has been laughingly described as "a blind person groping in the dark" or "feeling for fish in the water". How can one reconcile these perceptions with Chen Zhaokui's unequivocal statement that, "*I teach quan 拳 in order to teach combat*" and with Taijiquan's reputation as a fighting system *par excellence*?

First, one must appreciate that the slow pace of Taijiquan forms is a training method and not its aim. Records kept in Chenjiagou show that those achieving the highest levels of combat proficiency did so by following clearly laid down training standards and requirements. These criteria are precise, stringent and progressive. Beginning with the simplest requirements and progressing until the most complex. Taijiquan students have been passed down a systematic map of this training process. Zhu Tiancai, considered one of the elite Chen style practitioners today, explained: *"the requirements of shoufa 手法 (hand method), shenfa 身法 (body method) and bufa 步法 (footwork method) - from head to toe incorporating every joint of the body – each function has been transmitted orally by the ancestors".*

Once a student has understood the method, what they are actually training is agility and speed. Slowness *(man 慢)* is necessary to train correct body structure and in order to cultivate speed; softness and pliancy *(rou 柔)* is utilised in order to harness *"gang 刚"* steely strength; looseness (**松** *song*) is necessary in order to have elasticity and bounciness. This unique training method is described as smoothing out the meridians *(jingluo 经络)* for the free flow of qi to activate an individual's external movements. *"When the qi is full and abundant in the body, the strength becomes wholesome and unequalled. There will not be any obstruction in its path of transmission. There will not be any external stiffness to impede your movement and you can direct your harnessed strength to whichever part of the body you wish"* (Chen Zhenglei, 2003). It is the process of achieving a supreme state of looseness and pliancy so that the body's strength can be used fully and with optimum speed.

As a combative system, the practice of Taijiquan establishes a solid and stable lower plane *(xiapan 下盘)*, supple and agile upper body, and the body's intrinsic energy *(qi 气)* full and flowing (ready for use). Consequently, the trained exponent's movements appear smooth, natural and effortless. In ancient China numerous schools of boxing held to the superiority of circularity over linear movements. Chen Style Taijiquan follows the theory of using round movement to overcome an attack. The objection to linear movements was emphatically repeated in the majority of old boxing texts. This characteristic was particularly emphasised in methods of combat based upon the strategy of defence or counterattack. In Taijiquan an exponent does not clash head on with an opponent; instead, any attack is influenced tangentially after it has been fully launched. When an attacking force approaches, deflect the oncoming force (in Taiji parlance, this is known as leading into emptiness *"yin jin luo kong"* 引进落空), then utilise (borrow) the force to hit back *(jie li da ren* 借力打人*)*. No matter what form an opponent's attack takes, *"whatever comes in contact with your body, you deflect with a constantly rotating body – just like a rapidly spinning wheel, whatever touches it will ricochet away"*. (Chen Zhenglei, 2004)

While Chen Style Taijiquan includes many kicks and strikes within its arsenal, in essence it is a close range throwing and grappling system. The realities of combat necessitate that a practitioner be well versed and comfortable during close-quarter fighting. The system is renowned for its joint locking, throwing and takedowns all built on its unique coiling and spiraling energy.

An "Internal" Martial Art

Taijiquan is a sophisticated "internal" martial art. In order to achieve its ultimate skill, it is important to follow training criteria that are different from other martial arts. The internal aspects of Taijiquan are less obvious; they are subtle and cannot be trained or experienced in a short time. The internal is the source, the essence which is subsequently transformed to an energy that is then articulated externally by the body. However, before a practitioner can enter the door of internal training, it is important to have a clear understanding of what the term refers to.

An often-repeated Taijiquan maxim is, *"to train quan (boxing) and not train gong (skill), will come to nothing in the end" (lian quan bu lian gong, dao tou yi chang kong*

The Essence of Taijiquan 太極之粹

Chen Jun demonstrating Taijiquan's solid and stable lower plane (xiapan), supple and agile upper body, and the body's intrinsic energy (qi) full and flowing (ready for use).

Photo courtesy of Michael Vorwerk

练拳不练功，到头一场空). The *gong* denotes *gong li* or the internal aspect of martial strength. This saying cautions against concentrating on the external movements without paying attention to the accompanying internal substance. For example, postural changes that are not accompanied by a change in breathing, or a form performed without varying the tempo between stillness and movement means you have external movement without internal substance. As a starting point it can be said that internal strength is ensuring that the capacity you have within your body is co-ordinated with and complementary to your external movement.

At the heart of Taijiquan practice lie the three inseparable facets of movement, breathing and intention. A practitioner will not accomplish a holistic result if he does not pay attention to any of them. However, the training of these three aspects must be built on the base of a solid accurate foundation. The practitioner's emphasis changes depending upon the stage reached. During the preliminary stages of practice, greater importance should be placed on movements and not over-emphasis on the synchronisation of breathing and movement. Beginning students who place too much attention on this aspect inevitably compromise the accuracy of movements as well as the ease of breathing. Intention during the initial phase simply requires the learners to focus their minds on accurately memorising the movements. When the postures and transition movements are precise, one often finds that the breathing has naturally adjusted and can then begin to pay conscious attention to the coordination of breathing and movements.

Luihe - The Six Harmonies

Taijiquan is an all-encompassing study that requires the body to be understood as a unified whole, a system. As mentioned before, the main requirements of Taijiquan are looseness *(松song)*, pliancy *(柔rou)* and slowness *(man慢)*. Taijiquan's trademark slow training method facilitates enhanced co-ordination of the whole body and the ability to rid the body of

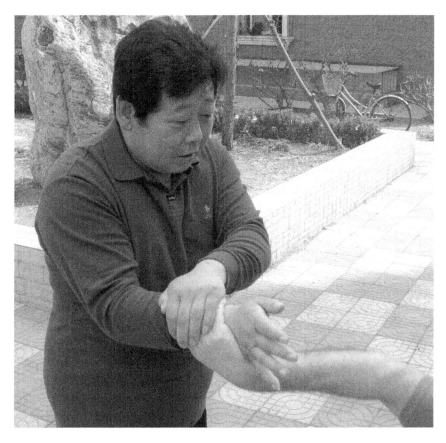

The powerful Qinna of Chen Yu is built upon the unique coiling and spiraling energy of Chen Taijiquan.

unnecessary tension. This can only be achieved after a prolonged and dedicated period of slow training. In the process a person also fosters a unification of body and mind, which is often described as the harmonisation of the mind (xin 心), intention (意 yi), intrinsic energy (气 qi), and body calisthenics (li 力). All aspects of an individual – physical, emotional, mental and spiritual – are thus interconnected and interdependent, and any single facet cannot be understood except in relation to the whole. This wholeness is achieved with the awareness of Taijiquan's "six harmonies".

The "six harmonies" encompass the "three external harmonies" *(waisanhe*外三和*)* and the "three internal harmonies" *(neisanhe*內三和*)*. To realise the three external harmonies all physical aspects of the practitioner's body must be arranged and structured in relation to each other. The three external harmonies generally represent the connections between the hands and feet *(shou yu zu he* 手与足和*)*, elbows and knees *(zhou yu xi he*肘与膝和*)*, and shoulders and kua *(jian yu kua he*肩与跨和*)*. These harmonies can be further extended to encompass the relations between the left hand and the right foot, the left elbow and the right knee and the left shoulder and the right *kua*跨 (and vice versa) etc. Feng Zhiqiang 冯志强, the most renowned student of 17th generation Chen Fake 陈发科 still living today, explained that the external harmonies could be understood as everything *"arriving at the same time"* – all actions executed as an integrated whole. The right way for a Taijiquan boxer to generate power in the execution of his techniques comes not from isolated muscular strength, but instead from a correctly aligned body structure and unified movement through a relaxed physical and mental state.

The three internal harmonies denote the unification of one's heart *(xin* 心*)* and intention *(yi*意*)*, the intrinsic energy *(qi*气*)* and the body's strength (力*li*), and the tendon *(jin*筋*)* and bone *(gu*骨*)*. To understand the concept of *xin* and *yi*, it is important to interpret its meaning. According to Chinese concepts, a person has an emotional mind *(xin*心*)* and a logical mind *(*意*yi)*. The literal translation of the Chinese character *xin* is "heart". Early pictograms of the character for *xin*, emblazoned on bronze inscriptions, unambiguously show a picture of the physical heart. *Xin* represents the centre of human feelings and emotions. Literature from the Warring States period of Chinese history depicts it as the centre of an individual's emotions and sentiments, from tranquillity and calmness, to anger, grief and disappointment.

Yi can be interpreted as "intention" or the logical mind. Fully focused energy can only be achieved with a decisiveness of purpose. Zhang Dainian (2002), Professor of Philosophy at Beijing University, explained: *"The intentions are the direction taken by the mind and the impetus to action".* Modern writers of Chinese use the term *yi zhi* 意志 to refer to the idea of "will" or "intention", and through the ages philosophers have emphasised the importance of tempering and marshalling the will to guide a person's conduct and approach to life. For example, Mencius 孟子 contrasting the will and qi asserted that: *"The will is the general of qi; qi is what fills the body. The will is first to arrive; qi follows. Thus it is said: "Maintain one's will and do no violence to one's qi".* Taijiquan practitioners are often instructed to *"yong yi, bu yong li* 用意不用力", translated as to *"use intention not force".*

In a combat situation conflicting feelings or thoughts can easily get in the way of achieving a successful outcome. To cultivate mental unity one must have present the emotional mind as well as the logical mind. One needs *xin* to summon morale and courage, and *yi* to make clear judgment and logical decisions. *Xin* without *yi* would mean fighting with emotion and a lack of clear thinking. *Yi* without *xin* would mean the lack of the fighting spirit although the intention is present. Connecting the heart and the intention enables an exponent to harness a fully focused and integrated energy. This is then combined with the powers of the body for a joining of internal and external aspects – that is the connection of energy and strength (qi and li). When this is achieved the body functions as a unified whole – that is linking the tendons with the bones.

Explaining the body's internal co ordinations, Zhu Tiancai wrote that the three connections combine in a chain reaction. *Xin* is first activated, for example, in instigating an action. The *yi* then dictates the direction and power of the action. *Yi* then sets in motion *qi* - energy – that, under the direction of yi, starts to move and consequently produces *li* or physical power.

Chen Zhaopi described the manifestation of the three internal and three external harmonies: *"when the upper body intends to move, the lower body will follow.*

When the lower body intends to move, the upper body will lead. If upper and lower body move, the middle section will synchronize. If the middle section moves, then the upper and lower body will harmonize". In this way it follows the Taijiquan tenet whereby *"if one part moves, every part moves and if one part stops, the whole body stops".* Ultimately the Taijiquan exponent seeks to unify internal and external strength by combining a complete integrated and fully focused energy with the physical capabilities of the body. "When you have realised the principle of internal and external harmonising and your internal energy flows without obstruction, then the whole *taolu* (套路 handform) naturally becomes round and lively, the internal energy follows the changes of the external movement and circulates. This type of internal energy within the body, which follows the external spiral movement of the body, is Chen Style Taijiquan's *chansijin* 缠丝劲 (silk-reeling energy)".

Form Training – The Blueprint for Martial Skills

Form training is the central component of Taiji training if one is to realise the full combat potential of the system. The traditional approach to developing fighting skills first emphasised a prolonged period of handform practice. The comments of past generations of adepts attest to its fundamental importance within the Taijiquan training curriculum. Chen Xin of the 16th generation of the Chen family exhorted Taiji students to, *"practice ten thousand repetitions, and you will come to understand Taijiquan."* Chen Fake陈发科, the creator of the Xinjia 新架 (New Frame) routines, was reputed to have practiced 30 repetitions a day throughout most of his life. In an article entitled *The Foundation of Taijiquan*, Ma Hong马鸿, a renowned Chen Taijiquan writer, recounted how Wu Style Taijiquan founder Wu Jianquan吴鉴泉was said to have asked his students to aim to do the handform ten thousand times in three years.

Through continuous repetitive training one acquires the correct postural framework, eventually realising and working the correct movement principles into the body. Once this is achieved, learning how to apply the techniques contained within the form will be far easier. At this stage when the mind wishes to move swiftly the body can react in an instant. Within the Taijiquan routines there are an almost unlimited number of potential

Chen Xiaoxing in Liu Feng Si Bi Posture – Form training is the central component of Taijiquan training if one is to realise the full combat potential of the system.

applications. 18th generation standard-bearer Chen Zhaokui 陈照奎 said, *"the practice of the form is the most important foundation work because the form is the end result of the accumulative fighting experience [of past generations of practitioners who used the techniques in real combat situations]. Most martial arts in their early stages are [made up of] only single postures. These postures grow in numbers, and eventually become a set or martial art form. Practicing the form will enable you to defend yourself in a fight"* (Ma Hong, 1998).

The form should serve as a template rather than a shackle. According to Chen Zhaokui every movement should be closely studied so as to be able to understand the many different martial applications contained within. Chen Zhenglei (1999) suggested that one should think of each movement in terms of the entire route. Even a movement like *Yan Shou Hong Quan* (Hidden Thrust Punch 掩手宏拳), which has a seemingly obvious martial application, can be used to deliver a punch, elbow strike or shoulder strike, depending upon at which point power is released. Throughout the routine one must consider the rationale behind each movement: whether it is used to neutralise or to attack; which intrinsic energy is being used – *peng, lu, ji, an* 掤捋挤按 etc.

At the highest-level Taijiquan is said to be formless, especially in terms of practical application. In response to the unpredictable and ever-changing conditions encountered when faced by an opponent, a Taijiquan adept must be capable of adjusting instantly and appropriately to the situation. Chen Xiaowang explains: *"Taijiquan has thousands and tens of thousands of changeabilities. Its techniques are rich and multi-dimensional. If one tries to remember by rote and memorises rigidly, he would not be able to learn or memorise in a lifetime. Only memorising movements would be like 'water without a source' or 'wood that does not derive from a tree'. Although Taijiquan is profound, in the end, 'ten thousand methods trace back to one principle'. "One action leads to all actions, surging through each part in sequence"*.

This process has been passed down for many generations. However, in recent times there have been many debates and discussions on the relative importance of the form as a foundation and on ways to speed up the

The Essence of Taijiquan 太極之粹

Chen Xiaowang (left) "You must be capable of adjusting instantly and appropriately to the situation".

training process. At their most extreme, some view form training as useless and little more than empty sets of flowery choreography. Others claim that by emphasising *zhan zhuang* 站桩 (standing pole) practice or push hands, the learner can understand Taijiquan's intrinsic energy more quickly. Today's practitioners should perhaps consider the validity and credibility of any new method, bearing in mind that the form was the training model developed and refined by individuals with first hand combat experience and has stood the test of time.

Psychological Attributes

A particular mental attitude must be developed if one is to be able to calmly face combat encounters. Sunzi 孙子, the famous Chinese military tactician, writing on *Strength and Weakness* said: "*Military tactics are like flowing water. Flowing water always moves from high to low, and military tactics always avoid the enemy's strong points and attack his weak points. Whereas the course of flowing water is decided by the different landforms, the way to win victory in a battle is decided by altering the tactics according to the enemy's changing situation".*

A combatant should possess calmness and mindfulness when facing an opponent and have no prejudgment regarding the unfolding situation. Aspects such as the direction and speed of an attack, the most appropriate distancing, and what techniques to use in response etc, are different in every instance. Calmness is the first requirement, and from calmness the ability to quickly assess the intention of an opponent and to adapt as the situation dictates. A practitioner well versed in the Taijiquan training curriculum has at his disposal a comprehensive repertoire of skills that have been trained into his body to be brought forth instantly and instinctively at the correct instance.

Sunzi: "Always avoid the enemy's strong points and attack his weak points"

*"Neither deviate from your instructions, nor hurry to finish. Do not force things. It is dangerous to deviate from instruction or push for completion. It takes a long time to do a thing properly. Once you do something wrong it may be too late. Can you afford to be careless? Follow with whatever happens and let your mind be free; stay centered by accepting whatever you are doing. This is the ultimate… It is best to leave everything to work naturally…" (Zhuangzi - Inner Chapters*庄子內篇).

The ability to calmly assess the situation also depends upon an individual possessing a degree of courage when facing an adversary. In his *"Important Words on Martial Applications*用武要言*"*, fourteenth generation standard-bearer Chen Changxing陈长兴 said: *"the terrified will never achieve victory. He who cannot examine the situation will never protect [himself]"* (Chen Xiaowang, 1990). Chen Zhaokui also emphasised the need for bravery, allied to excellent fighting skills: *"Fighting outcome is largely determined by courage. However, courage alone is not sufficient. Superior boxing skills are indispensable. A brave fighter with first-rate skills is a tiger with wings"*.

Taijiquan combat skill has at its core the idea of controlling the centre of an opponent. The skilled practitioner does not defend himself by parrying the kicks or punches of an opponent, but by parrying the opponent himself. Chen Changxing, writing several hundred years ago, cautioned against focusing too closely on the extremities and losing sight of the opponent's centre: *"Practice as if there is an enemy in front of you. When faced with an enemy, [fight] as if there is no opponent. If a hand comes in front of your face do not look at it, if an elbow approaches your chest, do not see it … Xin must take the lead. Yi must conquer the opponent. Your body must attack him, and your steps must pass through him"* (Chen Xiaowang, 1990).

Chen Zhaokui stated that: *"In combat the priority is to wipe out the enemy, to preserve oneself is only secondary. Only by defeating the enemy can one effectively preserve oneself"*. In a physical conflict many martial artists fail because they concentrate almost exclusively on their own technique rather than the actual situation. Generations of Chenjiagou boxers were highly experienced in real life and death combat situations, whether it be through warfare, employment as bodyguards or protecting their clan from bandits during lawless times. Chen Changxing painted a vivid picture of the necessary psychological approach:

> *"To get the upper hand in fighting, look around and examine the shape of the ground. Hands must be fast, feet light. Examine the opponent's movements like a cat. Mind must be organised and clear … If hands arrive and body also arrives [at the same instant], then destroying an enemy is like crushing a weed"* (Chen Xiaowang, 1990).

Chen Changxing's words reveal a practical approach that balances the physical and psychological aspects necessary to be successful in a combat situation. In modern times there has been a mystification of not just Taijiquan, but traditional martial arts as a whole. These arts that for centuries were trained in a practical and pragmatic way as a means of self-protection are treated like a modern science fiction.

For example, the skill of *qing gong* 轻功 (skill of lightness) dramatised in martial arts movies by warriors flying through the air, running across water and walking across snow without leaving any footprints, has led people to conclude that these skills are nothing more than fantasy. *Qing gong*, however, is a real skill that serious practitioners looking for total body conditioning would do well to cultivate. 18th generation exponent Chen Zhaoxu 陈照旭, the eldest son of Chen Fake and father of Chen Xiaowang, was said to have exceptional *qing gong ability*. Stories are still recounted in Chenjiagou of how he would effortless scale the high courtyard wall of his home as a shortcut to walking through the doorway. In reality, *qing gong* describes someone who are trained in the ability to jump higher than normal people, to *"borrow the strength from the ground".* They simply have more spring in their legs. A quick look at the many world-class high jumpers, hurdlers, basketball players etc shows that this ability is still very much alive today.

Modern day qing gong – agility training in the Chenjiagou Taijiquan School

Chen Wangting's Boxing Canon

The creator of the Taijiquan system Chen Wangting's Boxing Canon 拳经 is one of the earliest written records surviving in Chenjiagou and is the only preserved piece of his Taijiquan theories. Based on Qi Jiguang's 戚继光 Boxing Canon, it comprises of one hundred and fifty-four characters divided into twenty-two verses. In this short work he describes the fundamental nature of Chen style Taijiquan. There have been a number of interpretations for the verse, however, all agree that it is a profound piece of work and a good place for the serious Taijiquan exponent seeking insights into the art as it was practiced several centuries ago.

The verse allows practitioners to identify the distinctive qualities and specialities of Chen Style Taijiquan. At its heart the system emphasises martial effectiveness aligned to the economical exertion of strength - achieving victory through the use of skill rather than brute force; using trained softness to overcome hardness; making use of incoming strength to attack; and using the principles of physics to defeat an opponent.

"Releasing or extending no one can predict; reeling and coiling I simply comply.

Chopping, hitting, pushing and pressing to advance; shifting, intercepting, blocking and plucking too are difficult to defeat.

Everyone knows about hooking and warding to crowd and surround; but who knows about dodging and startling in order to take with deceit?

Feigning defeat and shamming retreat who says I've failed? leading and enticing to a sudden return to victory.

Rolling, dragging, bridging and sweeping are excellent; directly or obliquely chopping and cutting are even more wondrous.

Intercept and enter, cover and block as well as piercing heart with elbow; hasten the step like the wind is red cannon fist.

Double changing, sweep and press to circle the feet; left and right side entries to pin the legs.

The Essence of Taijiquan 太極之粹

*Bend forwards or press backwards without leaving an opening;
make noise in the east and attack in the West - know this well.*

Remember to net the top and lift the bottom; advance to attack and dodge to withdraw – do not hesitate.

There are many under the heavens who hide their heads and cover their faces; but those who pluck out the hearts and cut the ribs are scarce on earth.

Teachers who do not know this principle; will not be regarded in the martial arts."

拳经总歌

纵放屈伸人莫知，诸靠缠绕我皆依。
劈打推压得进步，搬摝横采也难敌。
钩棚逼揽人人晓，闪惊巧取有谁知？
佯输诈走谁云败？引诱回冲致胜归。
滚拴搭扫灵微妙，横直劈砍奇更奇。
截进遮拦穿心肘，迎风接步红跑捶。
二换扫压挂面脚，左右边簪庄跟腿。
截前压后无缝锁，声东击西要熟识。
上笼下提君须记，进攻退闪莫迟迟。
藏头盖面天下有，攒心剁肋世间稀。
教师不识此中理，难将武艺论高低。

Explanation of the verse

Releasing and extending refers to the strategy of enticing an unsuspecting opponent in to a vulnerable position. This requires a degree of courage to let an opponent come in to a seemingly advantageous position without resisting them, rather than keeping them at bay. It is like unleashing in order to draw in. The opponent should have no idea about one's intention; he is made to think that he has the upper hand and therefore confidently comes in to attack. However, behind the illusion of vulnerability is a clear intention. As the opponent enters the skilled exponent does not intercept and resist with force, but follows the momentum and then reacts according

Chen Wangting's Canon of Boxing preserved in the Chen Family Temple.

to the situation. This is achieved without anticipating the actions of the opponent, reading the variables of direction and force of an attack and changing and neutralising according to this force.

Adapt to an opponent's position and utilise his strength. *"Avoid the substantial and go into the insubstantial so that your own strength is not clearly visible. Sometimes an opponent discerns your force, sometimes he does not. Consequently he is not able to work out exactly where you are and feels unable to use any of his own technique and strength"*. Feeling an attacker's force an experienced practitioner should be able to neutralise in response without displaying any hint of resistance. As soon as there is resistance, the opponent can read it. If an opponent wants to go up, one must go even higher. If he wants to go down, follow him. When he advances, accept him so that he feels that *"the whip is long, but it does not go beyond you (reach you)* 鞭长莫及之. *And when he retreats, stay with him so that it is impossible for him to escape*退时即跟逼而上，使之难以逃脱".

To make a martial system become second nature, one must first master the *bufa*步法 (footwork) and *shoufa* 手法 (hand method) as well as the *shenfa* 身法 (a fully integrated body system), characterised by the close unison of movements. The footwork is the forerunner of an attack. The footwork and upper body must be synchronized or it will be very difficult to strike or capture an opponent effectively. In combat the agility and liveliness of footwork determine effective execution of defensive and offensive techniques, accuracy, distance, speed, strength, as well as reaction time and the overall quality of techniques. The importance of this point is captured in a number of Taijiquan sayings, examples of which include: *"if the hand arrives and the step does not move, the attack is bound to be late*手到步不移，打去必然迟"; *"if the hand arrives but the step does not, your strike will be ineffective*手到步不到，打着也不妙"; a third saying colourfully suggests that if *"hand arrives, foot arrives, even a jingang will fall*手到步也到，金刚也得倒" (The term *"jingang"* 金刚refers to the warrior guardian figure that often adorn the entrances of Buddhist temples.

Among the villagers of Chenjiagou the term is often used to refer to an unusually strong person); yet another saying unequivocally states that: *"it is no easy feat to closely synchronize your hand method and footwork – but once achieved an opponent will find it very difficult to defy or neutralise even simple techniques such as shifting, intercepting, blocking and plucking, let alone strong methods of attack such as chopping, hitting, pushing and pressing".*

When an opponent attacks, the usual response is to protect oneself by using the hands to block or grab. Or to pull or push in response. The success of this kind of response is dependent upon using superior size, strength and speed to counter the attack. These methods can be trained relatively quickly and are not considered as high skill in taiji terms. True martial skill does not depend upon using one's physical state to ensure victory. Instead, the skilled exponent relies upon the use of strategy and intelligence to defeat an opponent who might be bigger and stronger. Making use of the trained energies of *shan* 闪 and *jing* 惊 is a superior, sophisticated method that very few people actually master. *Shan* refers to Chen Taijiquan's method of dodging or getting out of the way of an opponent's attack. Usually this energy is executed with great speed and suddenness causing confusion to an opponent. *Shan* can be as straightforward as turning the upper body from the waist or stepping aside in order to avoid contact. The more complex method involves the use of *ting jin* 听劲 – 'discerning energy' - to perceive an attack and then to unexpectedly create a space between oneself and one's opponent. In the *Laojia Yilu* (Old Frame First Routine) *shan* energy is most obviously trained in the movements *Pie Shen Quan* 撇身拳 (Flinging Body) and *Shan Tong Bei* 闪通背 (Flash with Back).

To successfully use the strategy of *"feigning defeat and shamming retreat"* before *"leading and enticing to a sudden return to victory"*, one must present an impression of weakness to an opponent - perhaps even going so far as appearing ready to turn tail and run. This is a conscious battle strategy – pretending defeat to lure an opponent in, so that he becomes complacent and drops his guard. Then without warning you suddenly turn the tables and advance aggressively into him.

The Essence of Taijiquan 太極之粹

Chen Family Taijiquan was devised and later honed by individuals with real combat experience. Chen Wangting was a general in the Ming dynasty and is said to have carried with him the military strategy manuals of General Qi Jiquang and of Sunzi. The tactic of feigning weakness has many historical precedents on the battlefield. General Qi is most famous for his victories over the Japanese pirates （*Wokou* 倭寇）who terrorised China's coastline in the sixteenth century and resurgent Mongol attacks along the Great Wall. In both instances he engineered the conflicts in such a way as to neutralise the strengths of his enemies, lulling them into false sense of security and then turning to overwhelm them (Millinger and Fang, 1976).

Chen Xiaoxing in the movement Pie Shen Quan

The principle of *"leading an opponent into emptiness and then returning"* is one of the most fundamental fighting strategies of Taijiquan. In practice, skilled Taijiquan exponents seek to follow the opponent's direction of strength, and to combine their own strength with the opponent's force so that the two forces become one. Spiral and arc movements are then used to change the direction of the force. Once an individual masters the correct method of following and changing, then it really doesn't matter how big the incoming power is, as he will be able to neutralise it causing one's opponent to lose position. Leading into emptiness, therefore, is a means of controlling an opponent so that one's own strength becomes natural and an opponent's strength becomes awkward and in this way victory can be gained.

Chen Style Taijiquan uses a wide range of techniques such as *gun* 滚 (roll), *qian* 牵 (draw/drag in), *da* 搭 (bridge), *sao* 扫 (sweep), usually in combination with each other. *Gun* involves movements using fluid and agile circular rolling actions. The *jin* is often compared to a string of pearls, linked and joined together. When in contact with an opponent *gun* allows one to roll away with ease. Movements have the quality of being smooth and slippery so that the opponent cannot find a place to latch onto. A state of balance is required where one is always in the position of not resisting an opponent's actions and equally importantly not losing contact or "running away" from them. *Qian* uses Chen Taijiquan's characteristic spiralling action to draw in an opponent in a coil-like movement. Reeling inwards, the opponent's power can be neutralised so that he is unable to apply his intended technique. *Da* is the ability to bridge an opponent's power and direction in the instant in which you make contact – *"when the two hands meet"*. Then one can naturally extend or contract to avoid the incoming strength and follow the direction of the strength in order to neutralise it. Performed correctly, the opponent is placed either in a position where he cannot apply his strength or conversely is overly committed so that you can easily neutralise or fell him. *Sao* includes sweeping, tripping and hooking movements. It is usually a *tuifa* 腿法 (leg method) used in conjunction with the aforementioned three methods of *gun, qian* and *da*. The upper limbs are

used to control and close an opponent off and the legs are used to attack the lower limbs – hence *"remember to net the top and lift the bottom"*. While the opponent can be thrown with this technique, it can also be used to set up a finishing attack. By hooking an opponent's heel, his upper body becomes powerless and it is then simple to fell him with little effort.

"Intercept and enter, cover and block as well as piercing heart with elbow **截**进遮拦穿心肘*"* refers to the simultaneous combination of defence and attack. Even in the face of a committed attack by a powerful adversary one must guard against the advance without making the mistake of wrestling with strength. Take advantage of an attack and move boldly forward into an opponent's space; like a matador who defers to the bull and uses the animal's superior strength to bring about its defeat. At heart, Taijiquan is a close range combat system. As well as cover and block, one must also advance, close the distance with an opponent, adhere to his body and in that instance use the point of the elbow to strike into his heart.

By finding a gap to enter and counterattack an opponent without slowing the full advancing momentum the effect is like a head-on car crash, doubling the degree of impact. Except that the skilled exponent will strike their opponent's most vulnerable areas with their strongest point. This short-range method of attack usually utilises *zhou* 肘 and kao 靠, as in *chuan xin zhou* 穿心肘 (piercing heart elbow) and *ying men kao* 迎门靠 (head-on bump). *"Welcome the opponent's advance, step into the body, feel his jin and then attack"* - the most common mistake in trying to use this tactic is unleashing one's own counterattack too early. This tactic requires courage and confidence and the ability to literally look into the whites of an attacker's eyes before you commit your own response.

Besides the hand method one must also pay attention to the lower plane (*xiapan* 下盘), leg and foot techniques. Accurately determine appropriate timing and distancing for the effective application of one's own techniques. Watch out for the instant an opponent's weight changes or when he changes technique. Step in to 'welcome' an opponent's advance. This skill is known as *"hua xia ji shang"* 化下击上 or "neutralising beneath and attacking above". This can be applied in a number of ways. For example, the instant an opponent changes his weight or is changing technique, his support leg can be taken via a leg sweep. Or step and press his ankle joint or the back of the foot. Alternatively hook, sweep or kick the heel of the supporting foot in order to destroy his stability. One has to accurately judge the moment the foot is used. As soon as you have utilised the sweep, press or hook methods, you must rapidly follow up by entering the opponent's crotch area (*dang* 挡) or the inside of the thigh in order to lock and tie up the opponent's leg, foot and heel. When he is unable to advance or retreat couple it with the upper body's attack in order to fell him.

The effective application of one's techniques requires decisive and definite action with no hesitation or "gaps". Whether one is leading an opponent's *jin* into another path so that he falls into a void, or controlling his leg, in

Chen Xiaowang and Chen Bing demonstrating the practical use of Chen Taijiquan.

order to block his retreat and ability to change techniques must be executed instantly without wavering. This method is the successful utilisation of the technique *"forgoing oneself to follow others"* (she ji cong ren 舍己从人) : *"If an opponent wants to go to the left, I intentionally lead him to the left; if he wants to go to the right, I deliberately lead him to the right; if he wants to enter I welcome him in; if he wants to retreat, I follow his intention and retreat with him; if he wants to go upwards, I allow him to go up; if he wants to go down, I harmonise with his will".* Follow the opponent's *jin* so that he cannot fathom where the root is.

The ability to confuse an opponent by presenting him with confusing messages is an important fighting skill. The psychology behind this tactic is referred to as *"make noise in the east and attack in the west* 声东击西*".* For this tactic to be successful a real attack is hidden within a fake one. In an article entitled *Training for Sparring* Chen Zhaokui also used the expression *"make noise in the east and attack in the west".* He expanded upon this point, warning that if a feign attack did not look real, then the true attack was certain to fail. Therefore, every effort must be made to draw the opponent's attention to the fake attack. At the same time the real intention should not be given away by any telltale signs, e.g. facial expression etc: *"we can use the signs to confuse the opponent. For example, the first time you look at the left but strike from the right, then the second time you can look at the right of an opponent but strike from the right. The opponent after tasting the first fake strike will think the potential strike will come from the left this time. But he may get a punch from the right".* Chen Zhaokui described this as *"attacking where there is no defence".*

Taijiquan exponents are constantly reminded to use strategies and tactics rather than physical strength to defeat an opponent. For example, welcoming the opponent's attack by stepping up to bridge his incoming force; the use of *shan (dodge)* to nullify the approaching force of an opponent etc. This skill is based on the ability to trick and to bluff an opponent so that the opponent is deceived. For this to be successful requires not only combat ability but also mind cultivation, so that there is calmness and focus and the ability to make appropriate judgement and decisions even in the most stressful situations.

The final verses: *"There are many under the heavens who hide the heads and cover the faces; but those who pluck out the hearts and cut the ribs are scarce on earth. Teachers who do not know this principle; will not be regarded in the martial arts"* provide sound advice to all Taijiquan practitioners. Many people train in the martial arts but very few reach the highest levels. Concentrating on the superficial aspects of Taijiquan, collecting numerous forms without direction and aim, learning numerous applications without looking to the underlying rules, will result in a shallow understanding at best. Ultimate success is dependent upon a strong basic foundation built through careful study and rigorous training. Chen Xiaowang explained in plain terms that *"once you understand the postural and movement principles you understand all forms, weapons and applications. A thousand techniques return to one principle* 万法归一. *If you fail to understand this you are similar to a tree without roots* 无本之木 *or a river without a source* 无源之水. *You cannot grow"*.

San shou training in the Chenjiagou Taijiquan School

CHAPTER FOUR

OVERLAPPING STEPS

CHEN TAIJIQUAN'S PROGRESSIVE TRAINING SYLLABUS

David Gaffney & Davidine Siaw-Voon Sim

Chen Taijiquan's Progressive Training Syllabus

"Natural is the number one principle; progression in stages; when tired train in a high stance; when strong take a low stance; half the mind is concentrated, the other half set free"
— Chen Xiaowang

The different components of traditional Chen Taijiquan curriculum are interrelated and interdependent, and must be practiced to maximise the benefits of practice. From an individual's first contact with Chen Style Taijiquan, from training the standing pole, through the curriculum of basic exercises, progressing to form (hand and weapons) training, to push hands, until eventual mastery; the whole process should be approached in a systematic way. Learners often look at the skill level of the highest masters, people with fifty plus years of experience, and pessimistically assert that they cannot possibly achieve the same results. This is to fail to grasp that every one of these masters began as novices, and progressed through a clear and methodical syllabus. Zhu Tiancai, a leading teacher of Chen Taijiquan, compares a new beginner to a piece of blank paper with no content. *"Then you add to it bit-by-bit. You have no pressure - from simple to complex, from easy to hard, from superficial to deep - until you reach the highest level of Taijiquan gongfu. As you learn year-by-year putting in the necessary work you progress through levels of gongfu, having different realisations in each level".*

The traditional training curriculum handed down through generations of Chenjiagou Taijiquan exponents comprises of a number of diverse training methods. Each can only be understood when considered from within the framework of a systematic means of acquiring high-level martial proficiency. Chen Family Taijiquan is a logical and comprehensive system of martial art developed and perfected by military combat veterans. Examining Taijiquan in its birthplace Chenjiagou allows one to cut through inaccuracies and misinterpretations and experience the traditional ways of gaining skill that have been handed down from generation to generation since Chen Wangting陈王庭 (1600-1680) created the system nearly four centuries ago.

The benefit of studying the high philosophy underpinning Taijiquan is of limited use to a new learner, as it is too profound and complex to apply in a practical way. To be able to recite Taijiquan's complex theories and regurgitate whole verses from the Taijiquan classics is meaningless if it is not backed up by sustained training so that the principles of Taijiquan can be manifested physically and brought out at will. To increase the level of intellectual understanding and physical skill one must approach the different stages of training in a comprehensible manner.

Chen Taijiquan calls for the body to be used in a unique way. Like learning any new skill, it is necessary to start with the fundamentals. In time and with diligent practice, the body realises a new way of moving. The diverse training methods of Chen Style Taijiquan must be scrutinised within the framework of a larger structure. Each aspect of the training process from the seemingly simple standing practice to the intricate weapons forms and push hands drills is interrelated and necessary. Viewed as a whole, the progressive training route can be compared to a sequence of overlapping steps, each placed upon the supporting base of the preceding one. It is often said that all practice must be done *"according to the principles" (an zhe gui ju**按着**规矩)*. The principles begin with the basic requirements and develop step-by-step to the uppermost stages of expertise.

Using a modern analogy, learning Taijiquan is like installing a computer with hardware and software in order to improve its capability. The hardware increases the physical capacity of the computer, making it stronger and more functional. The software, on the other hand, performs the functions of the hardware and increases the number of functions. In order for a computer to perform increasingly complex tasks, it is necessary to continually upgrade both the hardware and the software. Taijiquan requires an exponent to possess a strong and useful body – the hardware, as well as trained skills – the software. Chen Ziqiang*陈自强*, a twentieth generation of the Chen Family believes that in order to become a good Taijiquan combatant a student must be proficient in four areas: *suzhi*素质 (constitution; the physical condition); *liliang*力量 (strength); *jishu*技术 (technical skill) and *gongfu* 功夫 (cultivated skill). It is not enough to put

Chen Ziqiang: Combat skills require good physical conditioning, strength, technical skill and gongfu.

emphasis on just one facet, or train isolated aspect of the system, whether it be softness, yielding or push hands. One must continually seek to improve and maintain the body's constitution (through good diet and correct lifestyle, for example) and at the same time increase the level of functionality (through persistent learning and training). Developing correct habits is a gradual process and the key is to have focus, patience and perseverance. All exercises within the curriculum are interconnected, each form are built on skills carried forward from another which are then added to the next, thus the combined effect of all learned skills is more important than learning individual techniques.

During the First International Advanced Chen Taijiquan Training Camp in Hebei province in China in 1999, Chen Zhenglei delivered a lecture on how to train Taijiquan correctly. He gave these guidelines for the acquisition of taiji gongfu: 1) learn Taijiquan's principles rather than train brute strength (*lian li bulian li*练理不练力); 2) train the source rather than its manifestation (*lian ben bu lian biao*练本部连标) and 3) train the body rather than the technique (*lian shen bu lian zhao*练身不练招) i.e. train the body to move as an integrated system rather than concentrating upon individual applications.

Many people take up Taijiquan believing it to be an 'easy' option having witnessed the seemingly soft and gentle manifestations of the Taijiquan forms. Some commentators are even known to say that the graceful movements of Taijiquan do not require any physical effort. This is a common misconception. The people in Chenjiagou have long accepted that the task of learning Taijiquan is a painstaking and challenging undertaking. However, Chen Style Taijiquan does not require beginning learners to start with complex techniques. Instead, the novice starts by looking to recognise and deal with fundamental body requirements and carry out basic body movements. Training is focused upon developing enough internal as well as external strength to carry out these actions.

Chen Xiaoxing: Low stances are the result of progressive training and are not necessary for beginning students.

Critics of Chen style Taijiquan often point to the low stances and complex movements taken by experienced exponents as evidence of the system's unsuitability for all but the strongest newcomer. However, this is to ignore the progressive nature of the traditional syllabus. Beginning students should not, for example, be too concerned with taking a very low stance, which may in fact be counter-productive. Taking up a posture that is too low can lead to knee injury and lead to the muscles becoming tense and rigid thus impeding qi flow. How demanding the training involves also depends on what a practitioner trains Taijiquan for – for general fitness, or for competition and combat, or purely for the pursuit of a complete system in order to explore its entire wonder.

Zhan Zhuang – Cultivating Stillness

"To train Taiji one must begin at Wuji"

Chen Xin (1849-1929)

Chen Xin's reference to *Wuji* 无极 (No Polarity) as the starting point of Taiji practice presents a valuable insight for the student looking to enter the door of Chen Taijiquan's traditional training curriculum. Wuji is characterised by stillness, but it also has movement, a dynamic element. When the movement accumulated to a critical level, then you have grand movement (极动*jidong*) (Feng Ziqiang in T'ai Chi Magazine [Vol. 24, No. 3]). The Standing Pole or *Zhan Zhuang*站桩, a balanced posture with arms at the sides of the body, is often used as a method of realising *wuji* and is a method familiar to many Chinese martial arts.

Zhuang Gong 桩功 (Pole Training) in its simplest form is practiced with the arms held in front of the body as if holding a large ball. Outwardly it seems as if little is happening; the practitioner is in fact deeply occupied in a range of actions and sensations. The natural rise and fall of the breath and the sensations within the body are being quietly monitored. The stationary position is held for a period of time whilst developing awareness of and maintaining the most efficient and relaxed structural alignment needed to hold the position. Prolonged practice of this simple and yet complex exercise enhances postural awareness and calmness of the mind, and also considerably strengthens core musculature upon which Taijiquan movements rely.

Zhuang gong can also be practiced using any of the end postures of the Taijiquan form. The whole Taijiquan form movements, in fact, are often referred to as *huo zhuang*活桩, translated as 'movable pole', and therefore encompass the same fundamentals. A common internal martial arts adage states: *"if you have no stillness, you will not see the wonder of moving"*. Chen Xiaowang refers to this as the *"one posture principle"*.

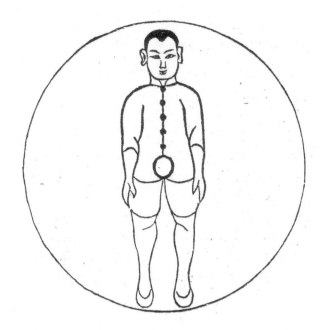

Illustration of *wuji* from Chen Xin's *Illustrated Explanation of Chen Family Taijiquan*

Taijiquan is an internal martial art, requiring internal energy *(neijin 內劲)* cultivation alongside external physical training: "*External training is to strengthen the tendons, ligaments and bones. Internal training is to strengthen the qi*". The power and strength of internal energy are apparent in external actions. A prerequisite to training internal skill *(neigong 內功)* is in its internal preparation, which includes the cultivation and storage as well as the circulation of *qi* (i.e. to manipulate it so that it can be controlled by one's intention).

Neigong training, therefore, requires quietness as its first principle. It is only in a quiet state that one is able to concentrate on the intent. This concentration determines the quality of internal training. *Zhan zhuang* cultivates the mind, qi and spirit, conditions the body and improves qi circulation so that it can be mobilised and coordinated with physical movements. In qi manipulation, the use of intention is the most important aspect. The stronger the intent, the greater is the outcome.

The Essence of Taijiquan 太極之粹

Therefore internal quietness *"should not be cut off all thoughts. Just collect the mind and don't let it go and get involved with idle thoughts. Then the mind will be profoundly unoccupied and naturally concentrated. When something happens it will respond accordingly (Zhu Xi朱熹)"*.

As *Zhan Zhuang* does not involve complex movements it is relatively 'easier' for the practitioner to concentrate the consciousness. Lessening the amount of external stimulation enables the practitioner to be attuned to feelings within the body. In time it leads to heightened body awareness as the practitioner discovers that as the outer body remains motionless, within, the breath, blood and qi are continuously moving. In this state, the experienced practitioner embodies a position of balance referred to in the Taiji classics as *"motion in stillness"*.

When asked what he believed is the most important principle within Chen Taijiquan, nineteenth generation standard-bearer Chen Xiaowang responded: *"Posture and position. The Standing Pole exercise is the first form. This readies the body for Taijiquan practice. Before you can drive a car you must first adjust the mirrors, seat position, seatbelts, etc. This exercise is similar. The dantian丹田 should be thought of as the centre. The body should be balanced, the mind quiet and peaceful, energy flowing everywhere throughout the body. The most important point is that the body is connected and the dantian qi is flowing and communicating with the rest of the body"*.

The process of prolonged internal training bring manifold results: the mind is quiet yet alert; there is acute lightness and sensitivity in the upper body whilst concurrently a sense of extreme weightiness and connection to the ground in the lower body; qi energy becoming fuller and stronger, saturating the energy centre in the lower abdomen *(dantian丹田)*, breaking through blockages in the energy paths *(jingluo经络)* and then filling the entire body. The body in this state is often likened to an inflated ball, filled with elasticity and brimming with a physical feeling of inner to outer expansion and strength *(peng jin 掤劲)*. By means of the spiraling "silk-reeling" movement of Chen Taijiquan, this energy can be circulated throughout the body. The combined effort of *zhuang gong 桩功*, accrued from *zhan zhuang*, form practice and in push hand should be natural with the body correctly aligned and relaxed. In this way the whole body (and mind) is trained to move as an integrated unit. The same Taijiquan principle is maintained during the forms, push hands and actual combat.

The internal training required of Taijiquan and other internal martial arts is often dismissed by some as some kind of esoteric practice. However, it is interestingly to note that many elite level mainstream sports coaches now acknowledge the critical importance of the "inner world" of the athletes under their charge. None more so than top sports psychologist James Loehr, who has trained world-class athletes in many different sports, who asserts that in the final analysis even the thoughts inside an individual's head must be considered as a physical aspect to be rigorously trained if they are to achieve excellence in their chosen discipline: *"This may sound quite shocking coming from a psychologist, but all the evidence is there. The body is physical; talent and skill are physical; emotions are neurochemical events and are therefore physical; and thinking and visualising are electrochemical events in the brain and are also physical… let's get it straight once and for all: thoughts and feelings are physical stuff too; they are just as real and every bit as fundamental to achievement as talent and skill"* Loehr, 1995).

Facing page: Zhan zhuang training in Chenjiagou – students are taught to first recognize and deal with fundamental body requirements.

The Essence of Taijiquan 太極之粹

How to Practice Zhan Zhuang

Stand with your feet shoulder width apart. Balance your weight evenly between both legs. Bend your knees slightly by relaxing the hips and keep the crotch slightly rounded. Feel your weight sinking down to your feet *(chengen沉根)*, taking care not to allow it to rest on the knees.

Keep your head up with the muscles of the neck relaxed and very gently extended. Feel the crown of the head reaching upwards as the chin tucks in slightly *(xuling dingjin虚领顶劲)*.

Lightly close your lips and bring the teeth together. Relax the jaw and rest your tongue lightly on the upper palate just behind your teeth.

Centre the coccyx *(weilu zhongzheng尾闾中正)* and relax the waist in order to keep the spine and the body straight *(lishen zhongzheng立身中正)*. [Therefore lining up and connecting the *baihui*白会, located on the top of your head, and *huiyin*会阴, located between the anus and perineum. It also allows the opening of the *mingmen*命门, located between the second and third vertebra – all to facilitate opening of meridians and qi flow].

Keep your *kua*胯 (the fold on top of your thigh) relaxed throughout *(songkua松胯)*.

Keep the legs full. Relax the ankles and feet. The toes lightly grip the ground –keeping the centre of the foot free (gently lift up the *yongquan*涌泉 or *bubbling well*).

Inhale and raise your arms in front of your body then exhale as you round them to form a circle in front of your body, as if you were embracing a large tree.

With awareness focused on the dantian, allow your thoughts to settle down and become quiet. Stand naturally upright and let the whole body go loose *(fangsong放松)*. Maintain a sense of listening to a point behind *(erting beihou耳听背后)*.

Chen Xiaowang in the normal stance used when training Zhan Zhuang

Breathe naturally *(huxi ziran 呼吸自然)*. Do not intentionally use your nose, mouth or lower abdomen to breathe (in order to avoid many of the problems associated with improper breathing. A common mistake is to attempt to deliberately push the breath down. Abdominal breathing cannot be forced; instead it should be allowed to develop naturally with regular practice).

Let half your intention be focused on the exercise and the half be free.

Maintain the position of deep relaxation and correct body requirements. Make slight adjustments if any part of the body feels stiff and tense.

Zhan Zhuang can also be trained in a lower position to develop lower body strength if the practitioner's strength allows it. It is of no benefit to train in the lower position if one has to compromise on the other postural requirements to do so.

The Essence of Taijiquan 太極之粹

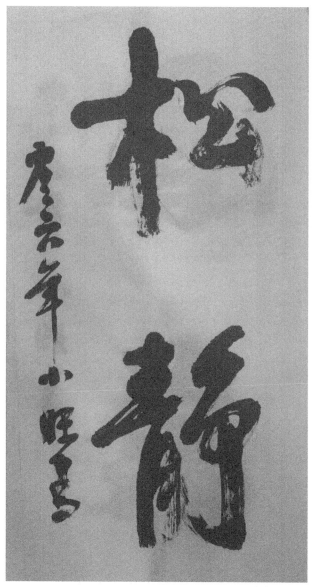

Calligraphy by Chen Xiaowang: "Song Jing" or "Relaxed and Quiet".

Chansigong: Silk Reeling Exercises

*"To understand Taijiquan you must understand spiral force.
If you do not understand, you do not know Taijiquan"*
— Chen Xin

One of the unique features of Chen Style Taijiquan is its use of *chansijin* 缠丝劲 or silk reeling force. Every posture, every action, and every technique is characterised by a spiral-like momentum that originates from the d*antian*. It is a method of body mechanics that is based on postural alignment and abdominally generated action that facilitates whole body movement. The waist is the primary pivotal axis and source of all movements. The importance of the waist is emphasised in the Taiji classics in a number of sayings, for example: *"If your waist does not move, do not move"* and *"if the inside (dantian) does not move, the outside should not move"*.

Silk reeling exercises or *chansigong* 缠丝功 provide a means of practicing Chen Taijiquan's unique method of movements and basic body mechanics through the repetition of individual movements. These exercises help one to progress further in the training curriculum from the standing exercise. From the central equilibrium acquired through static posture, the controlled spiralling of the body and limbs in *chansigong* help the circulation of energy (qi 气) and the development of power (*jin* 劲), and also helps to loosen and open up the major joints of the body.

When a practitioner performs the form – as he completes one action and then move on to another action- the postures are often designed to train a different skill or aspect of body mechanics. While many movements are repeated, they are spaced apart from each other within the sequence and, therefore, are not practiced continually. The silk reeling exercises comprise of individual movements, the mechanics of which make clear the basis for

one or more movements contained within the form. They provide a method by which to control energy distribution and to train the pathway of

The spiral force of Chen Taijiquan. Mural in the Chen Family Temple.

utilising *jin* 劲 or trained power. In silk reeling exercises, the spiral movements must be smooth and continuous so that the energy and power are uninterrupted. Silk reeling exercises link the practitioner's body sectionally from joint to joint until the body becomes an integrated whole and whole body power can be mustered.

The trained spiral motion has a number of practical functions. The soft coiling feature within the exercise facilitates the ability to stick to an opponent closely and securely. This ability is referred to as *zhannian* 沾黏 or sticking and adhering. The spiral movement also makes it possible to neutralise an incoming attack by deflecting and redirecting it away from oneself, or *"leading an opponent into emptiness"*. When hard, the spiral quality of Chansijin enables the use of any part of the body for attack. The trained body becomes impenetrable, warding off and rebounding any incoming force. A thorough knowledge of silk reeling movement is also essential if a practitioner is to access the extensive repertoire of *qinna* 擒拿 (joint-locking) applications concealed within the system, as well as developing the capacity to escape from joint locks.

Above and facing page: Chen Ziqiang demonstrating Zhengmian Chansi – Frontal Reeling Silk

The hand traces a circle going no higher than the eyebrow and no lower than the groin.

Shuangshou Chansi – Double Handed Reeling Silk

Rotating the crotch (*dang*) and the waist (*yao*), the whole body moves as a single unit.

Qianhou Chansi – Forward and Backward Reeling Silk

Ward-off (*peng*) upwards in an arc towards the front, then divert (*lu*) towards the rear.

David Gaffney & Davidine Siaw-Voon Sim

Barehand Forms – The Foundation of Chen Taijiquan Skills

"like flowing water and drifting clouds, continuous without break"

Chen Xiaowang

Forms training traditionally provides the foundation of Chen Taijiquan's systematic training curriculum. It is the principal conditioning method for providing the basic building blocks of the art, training practitioners to internalise a wide range of boxing techniques through the focused repetition of a prescribed set of movements. Form training is demanding and requires the total attention and participation of a person's mind and body. Elements such as patience, determination, strength, relaxation, *yi* (mind intent 意) and qi are crucial in honing one's Taijiquan skills. The original art devised by Chen Wangting was made up of five barehand boxing routines that were handed down for the next five generations. Chen Changxing 陈长兴 (1771-1853), the fourteenth generation standard bearer combined the five routines into the two *Laojia* 老架 (Old Frame) routines still trained today. These are the First Routine (*Yilu* 一路) and the Second Routine (*Erlu* 二路), also known as the *Paochui* 炮捶 or Cannon Fist form.

Chen Xiaoxing 陈小星, Principle of the Chenjiagou Taijiquan School, asserts that *"the synthesis of the five routines did not represent the loss of the original forms but of amalgamating the five, absorbing the essence of each. The First Routine and the Cannon Fist contain the same essence as the original routines, preserving many of the movements and all of the movement principles"* (Chen Xiaoxing, 2004). The Chen style Taijiquan barehand forms today are most often drawn from two main "frames": Old and New (*Laojia* and *Xinjia*, respectively). Seventeenth generation master Chen Fake 陈发科 developed the New Frame when he left Chenjiagou to teach in Beijing in 1928. Characteristics of the New Frame include more apparent silk-reeling movement; a greater number of power releasing actions and an increased emphasis on *qinna* 擒拿 (joint-locking) techniques. Both Old and New Frame comprise of a First and Second Routine; the First Routine with more emphasis on slow soft

Chen Xiaoxing: Forms training traditionally provides the foundation of Chen Taijiquan's systematic training curriculum.

movements whilst the Second Routine primarily trains fast and powerful movements.

Many practitioners often debate on whether the Old or New Frame is better? However, whether one practices the Old Frame or New Frame should not be the crucial question. Rather, it should be whether the form can successfully translate the principles of the system to the learner. In Chenjiagou and with the leading teachers of Chen Style Taijiquan, the Old Frame is usually held to represent the hard gained legacy of many past generations of adepts. It is considered to be a movement map used in conjunction with oral transmission, that preserves the painstaking method through which the skill has been handed down to subsequent generations up to the present time. Modern forms have to be judged against the criteria of whether or not they maintain the traditional essence and principle.

In Chenjiagou the Old Frame First Routine is usually the first form taught to students. *"This routine has unique characteristics; movements are comfortable and expansive, seeking softness through looseness. Within softness there is firmness, alternating fast and slow, combining hard and soft. The frame is comfortable and natural; the footwork is light and nimble and yet steady and stable. The body is naturally upright. Qi movement and jin route are like flowing water and drifting clouds, continuous without break. When emitting power the jin is loose, lively, springy and vibrant, completed in one breath"* (Chen Xiaowang – Zhonghua Wushu magazine 中华武术杂志).

The form is often likened to an educational syllabus that teaches the student to understand the complexities of the art little by little over time. During the learning process, emphasis is placed upon progressively adjusting one's physical state and in the process gradually elevating one's overall skill. The form should be understood as a framework or blueprint that must be correct if the practitioner is to realise the correct principle. For this reason it is essential to be instructed by a good teacher. First the learner must seek, by modelling the movements of a teacher, to standardise his movement as closely as possible with the basic requirements laid down for each part of the body. Each of the requirements is there for a reason, having practical implications for preserving good health, for making movements more efficient, for qi circulation, and for increasing the effectiveness of martial applications.

The Essence of Taijiquan 太極之粹

The Old Frame First Routine is often referred to as the *"gongfu frame 功夫架"*. With persistent and diligent training it allows an individual to begin to understand and to apply many of the important core principles of the system. The new learner must completely familiarise themselves with every movement of the form. This important stage must not be neglected as it lays down good habit and accuracy in terms of posture and the placement and movement of each joint of the body. Work to clearly understand Taijiquan's criteria for hand actions, body method and footwork, for example, the correct way to shape the hands; the precise way of stepping and basic footwork; awareness of how to wield the arms; and the basic way of turning the circle. In the beginning, therefore, most traditional teachers put most emphasis upon understanding the intricacies of each movement. This stage is called *"huadao'er 画道儿"* or *"plotting the route"*. During this period the teacher will constantly adjust a student's postural frame until a time when they are fully conversant with all the body requirements.

"During my training with Grandmaster Chen Zhaopi, he would keep stressing to us the importance of Laojia Yilu as the quintessential skill-building routine. He would emphasize that within its predominantly gentle focus; it contains an inherent force…this was how our ancestors passed down the skills to us from generation to generation…" (Zhu Tiancai 朱天才)

The Old Frame First Routine helps to instill the three characteristics of *song* 松 (looseness), *yuan* 圆 (roundness), and *rou* 柔 (pliancy). *Song* means not using stiff force. Many practitioners of Taijiquan will probably have been exhorted repeatedly to look for the quality of *fangsong* 放松 or to let loose. Western texts often translate the term simply as "to relax", which fails to capture the energetic state that is actually required. The renowned Taijiquan historian Gu Luixin 顾留馨 describes this state as one of the essential features of Chen style Taijiquan. He explained: *"…you require looseness (song 松) to get pliancy (rou 柔), and then softness to get hardness (gang 刚). From hardness you need to be able to revert to softness. So the goal is to simultaneously have softness as well as hardness and to be able to alternate hardness and softness".*

A student's posture is constantly adjusted until they are fully conversant with all the body requirements.

Yuan requires one to be aware of the centreline of the body and to use this as a movement boundary. The centreline can be understood as a line running from the nose to the navel. When turning the hand to push to the side, the hand pushes away from the centreline no higher than the eyebrow. As the hand draws in it does not pass the centreline and does not go below the crotch (*dang*裆). In this way circularity is maintained throughout the movement. *Rou* is the quality of elasticity and the absence of inflexibility and rigidity.

New students usually experience an inability to be loose or are not familiar with Taijiquan's method of loosening the body. Consequently, when performing explosive movements within the form such as *YanShou Hongquan* 掩手宏拳, *Qinglong Chushui* 青龙出水, *Dangtoupao* 当头炮,

*Shuangbaijiao*双摆脚 etc, the force they emit is stiff and awkward and they are unable to transfer whole body power to the extremities in an efficient manner. This is quite normal and can be overcome through an extended period of focused training until one gradually gains insight into the various requirements for each part of the body.

End postures within the form such as *Lanzhayi* 揽扎衣 *(Lazily Tying Coat)* or *Danbian*单鞭 *(Single Whip)* offers an opportunity for adjustment and correction in line with Chen Taijiquan's requirements for each part of the body. Most Taijiquan players are aware of the requirements, as they have been extensively written/spoken about; it is the degree that is difficult to appreciate. For example, most experienced Taijiquan practitioners would recognise the instruction to store their chest (*hanxiong*含胸), but how do you achieve this in practice? If you store excessively, the waist collapses, but then what is considered excessive? It is not like a project whereby someone just hands you a set measurement to work with.

"Only through persistent practice and strict adherence to correct principles can one achieve a stage where one is able to produce just the right amount of jin, change at will, and rotate with ease. One has to train hard in form practice so that the body becomes one single unit, which enables one movement activating all movements" (Chen Xiaowang, 1990).

This view is shared through the generations of Chen Family masters. Chen Fake of the 17th generation also said: *"beginners should practice slowly, so that the movements are correct. Practice makes perfect, so after a long time movements can naturally be fast and steady; when fighting the speed of the movements is dependent upon the opponent's speed; practicing slowly is the method to learn the boxing, but it is not the goal. However, when movements are slow, the legs are exercised for a longer time, which is also beneficial"* (Hong, 1998).

The logic behind Chen Taijiquan's customary emphasis on the First Routine as the foundation form lies in the characteristics of the form. The relatively slower and softer nature of the form allows a player to focus on the fine points; to ensure that postures are accurate; to assess stability and balance during movements; to develop lower body strength; and to become mindful of qi flow throughout the body.

To begin with the external form is used to lead internal energy. Form training is Chen Taijiquan's method of circulating and managing qi – to guide and focus the mind and the body's intrinsic strength to particular areas of the body as is required. Once an individual has acquired some sensation of qi, i.e. able to feel a concentration of energy which is commonly manifested as warmth, tingling, or a feeling of expansion etc through exercises such as *zhanzhuang* or *chansigong*, if they do not know how to direct it, it is still problematic. For instance, many beginners will not be able to perform the explosive movements within the Laojia Yilu (Old Frame First Routine) correctly as they have not yet been able to harness all the body's energy into a single point at the precise moment of execution. Interestingly, the Chinese word for strength "*li qi* 力气" literally means "*strong qi*". What is missing with most Taijiquan practitioners is not qi, but the method to concentrate and co-ordinate this intrinsic energy in order to emit it. This is why traditional teachers are so stringent in their requirement of ever more precise posture and movement in the form as this is the means by which the student will ultimately be able to focus their energy to the exact point where it is needed. To blindly train explosive movements without embracing the principle of practice will not yield the desired effect. The accuracy of the postures and movements within the form determines whether the qi is managed correctly. In a correct posture energy can be properly harnessed before emission. Too many practitioners concentrate on emissions (*fa*发) and neglect cultivation and storage *(xu*蓄).

Qi feeling varies with different postures and different movements. Chen Style Taijiquan's qi training method basically means that at all times one's posture and movement should be round, smooth and supported. The real skill of Taijiquan is not measured by how much an individual can shake his body or by how loudly he can stamp his foot. For generations Chenjiagou boxers have looked to achieve four maxims: "*zhannian liansui* 沾黏连随" (stick, connect, adhere, follow); "*wuguo buji* 无过不及" (neither over-extending nor not reaching far enough); "*budui buding*不丢不顶" (not losing and not resisting); "*yinjin lekong*引进落空" (leading into emptiness).

The alternating use of fast and slow movements is a unique feature of Chen

The accuracy of the postures and movements within the form determines whether the qi is managed correctly.

Style Taijiquan. A skilled exponent gathers energy slowly, but discharges power explosively. As to whether it is better to practice Taijiquan slowly or quickly, Chen Zhaopi stated that *"it is not a question of speed, but for the form not to be dispersed during fast actions and not to be broken during slow movements"*. Expanding upon this he explained that *"fast but not dispersed"* means that when an individual performs fast or explosive movements, the body's external shape (*waixing* 外形) is fully corresponding with the internal energy (*neiqi* 内气). *"Use internal energy to prompt the external shape so that shape is stimulated by qi and therefore qi and shape 'arrive' at the same time"*. Therefore, fast movements within the form executed in this way are correct. However, for people who have not reached a sufficient skill level to accomplish internal and external co-ordination, fast practice is not useful.

Conversely, the quality of slow movements in Taijiquan is *"slow but not broken"*. The breathing should be comfortable and natural during slow practice. If the pace is overly slow, not only are movements and breathing not co-ordinated, but it will not be possible to *"complete an action in one breath* 一气呵成". In training the form, using the correct movement principles, one movement follows another without break. Even when the external shape appears to have stopped the internal energy and mind's intention do not stop – *"xingduan jinbuduan*形断劲不断, *jinduan yibuduan*劲断意不断". Therefore, slow movements should not be lifeless and collapsed. Note the Taijiquan classics that say *"externally like a virgin, internally like a jingang*外如处女, 内似金刚". Chen Zhaopi wrote: *"If you make the mistake of being top heavy and bottom light; externally scattered and internally empty; wielding the arms and not the body; body and qi failing to arrive at the same time; qi and shape not together – like a plate of loose sand – then practicing slowly in this manner is not correct."*

An often-repeated axiom is that a form must be practiced at least 'ten thousand times'. It simply means that many repetitions are required for the form to become natural and effortless. Chen Fake was reputed to have practiced the form a minimum of thirty times a day throughout his life. His grandson, Chen Xiaoxing陈小星, principle of the Chen Village Taijiquan School, often speaks of the necessity of gaining attainment through *"grinding out the skill"* with endless repetitions of the forms.

When a person reaches an appropriate level of skill he can start training the Second Routine form (also known as *paochui*炮捶) to increase the ability to emit explosive power (*baofali*爆发力) as well as to develop endurance and stamina (*naili*奈力). Taijiquan is constructed upon the scheme of softness and hardness complementing and alternating with each other. As a result, the two routines embody a comprehensive balanced system of hardness and softness. The second routine form is performed at a faster pace and is physically challenging with many movements that involve power release (*fajin*), and practices leg sweeps, elbow and shoulder techniques and rapid changes between attack and defense. *"Where the first routine provides the means of developing internal energy, the second routine consolidates and expresses this energy"* (Chen Xiaoxing, 2004).

The different combat possibilities contained within each movement are also taught. This process is reflected in an often quoted Taijiquan saying: *"from*

The Essence of Taijiquan 太極之粹

David Gaffney in Lan Zha Yi (Lazily Tying Coat) Posture

familiarity to gradually realising and understanding jin". Although it is not strictly necessary for those who practice Taijiquan for health and for keeping fit to learn its combat application, knowledge of practical usage augments the accuracies of postures, giving basis and meaning to each action. The effectiveness of a particular posture is tested out in push hands *(tuishou*推手*)* drills, and gradually the practitioners reduce mistakes in movements and rid themselves of any compromising postures.

The impatient learner is often disheartened, or even disbelieving, when told that if they really want to develop effective Taijiquan fighting skills, it is better not to concentrate solely upon the applications when training the form but to give all their attention to building a sound postural framework. Taijiquan classics requires one to *"use the mind to direct the qi and use the qi to drive the body" (yixin xingqi, yiqi yunshen* 以心行气*,* 以气运身*)*, using spiraling and reeling motions to drive the energy in one's body into movements. Through adherence to correct principles and under good instruction, the body becomes capable of great changeability and flexibility, and able to adjust according to circumstances, equally conversant with both defence and attacks. If a person limits himself within prescribed techniques, it will severely affect his potential to achieve true skills.

Chen Xiaowang said: *"The purpose of learning Taijiquan form is for its fighting skill. If the body's frame allows one to suitably deal with the attacking nature of push hands, then it is evidence that the frame has been trained correctly. A person can then progress confidently to the next stage of gongfu".* The Taijiquan form should, therefore, be the core of one's daily training; everything else - push-hands, weapons forms, and power training exercises etc - being supplementary.

Tuishou – To Know one's Opponent

"Nobody knows me, while I know everybody"

Chen Wangting (1600 – 1680)

Training the forms without paying attention to the underlying function ultimately results in nothing more than a series of empty movements. In his creation of Taijiquan Chen Wangting陈王庭 was greatly influenced by one of the chapters of Qi Jiguang's 戚继光 Canon of Boxing which states that *"once you have the skill you must try it on your enemy, but you must guard against feeling dejected when you lose or complacent when you win. You must constantly consider why have you won or why have you lost? Have you lost because of fear of your enemy or because your skill is not deep enough. Because the ancestors always say the person of high skill must have a big gall大胆 [must be very brave]"*. After a period of research and assimilation of different methods he created Tuishou推手 (Push-hands) as a way of training fighting skills using Taijiquan principles but without incurring injuries to the practitioners. This represented a unique development in the history of martial arts training.

The practical experience achieved from push hands training provides immediate feedback to help validate the correctness of the form. Mistakes in the form will be quickly unveiled as mistakes in push hands. Push hands training is central to developing effective combat skills in Chen Taijiquan. It develops appropriation of *jin*, heightens sensitivity and trains stamina and endurance.   In the past the exercise was called hitting hands or *da shou* 打手. Almost all traditional Chinese martial arts use one of these five combat techniques: *ti* 踢 (kicking) *da* 打 (striking) *shuai* 摔 (wrestling) *na* 拿 (grasping) and *die* 跌 (felling), with different system having its own specialism. These specialism of techniques are illustrated in sayings such as *"nanquan beitui* 南拳北腿*"* (Southern fist, Northern leg) and *"changquan duanda* 长拳短打*"* (long fist, short strike).   Martial arts historian Gu Liuxin 顾留馨 (1998) suggested that these sayings signified the degree of specialism that had evolved within the different martial systems. He further pointed out that training methods that emphasised the techniques of kicking, striking, grasping and felling inevitably carried a high degree of risk to the participants. Over time many of these systems evolved into elaborate simulations of combat. As a result, although much time and effort was spent on study, because of the difficulty involved in training actual applications or techniques, it was very difficult to raise the standard of combat skill. Chen Wangting created *tuishou* to address this problem, basing the exercise on the core characteristics of coiling (*rao* 绕), spiraling (*chan* 缠), sticking (*zhan* 粘) and following (*sui* 随).

The current Chen Family Gatekeeper 掌门人 Chen Xiaowang 陈小旺 (1990) explains that the object of pushing hands is to achieve sensitivity to the movement and intention of an opponent, whilst disguising one's own intention and energy. Reaching this finely tuned level of sensitivity has long been the aim of Chen Taiji exponents. In the *"Song of the Canon of Boxing* 拳经总歌*"*, Chen Wangting states that one should seek to accomplish a level of ability where *"nobody knows me, while I know everybody* 人不知我，我独知人*"*. Harmonising with the movements of an opponent, the practitioner seeks to get rid of all tension and resistance within his own reactions. A number of benefits arise from loosening the joints and maintaining softness during push hands. Firstly it allows the practitioner to "stick" or adhere to an opponent more easily upon making contact. Sensitivity to another's movement is heightened enabling an individual to follow an opponent more closely, with more time to discern the opponent's *jin* and to react with an appropriate response. Distinct from most external martial arts, the aim is not just to overcome an incoming force with a greater force, but instead to "listen" to and "borrow" the opponent's energy to defend oneself. Sunzi孙子, the great Chinese military strategist wrote that: *"To secure ourselves against defeat lies in our own hands, but the opportunity to defeat the enemy is provided by the enemy himself".*

'Listening' skill *(tingjin*听劲*)* does not rely solely upon the practitioner's sense of touch, but involves whole body awareness. Some individuals turn the face away or shut the eyes while practicing, but really there ought to be total body consciousness, combining and coordinating all the senses including sight, hearing and touch.

Tuishou has long been used as a means by which to validate the correctness of the form. It allows the practitioner to put to the test the body postures trained in the forms. Correct body alignment enables one to control others and yet prevent others from entering one's boundary. It is said that all the ills in the form will be magnified and manifested in push hands, giving an opponent the opportunity to take advantage. For example, if one is easily uprooted during push hands, this may be symptomatic of stances or postures that are incorrect; if you find that an opponent is able to repeatedly borrow your energy to apply his techniques, then you must consider the possibility that you are applying force inappropriately in the first place and allows the opponent to capitalise on the mistake. Ineffectively executed movements in general signify a lack of co-ordination throughout the body. Therefore during push hands practice, one should not overlook any of the body requirements emphasised during form practice.

"Tuishou and form training are inseparable. Whatever defect a person has in the form will be revealed during push hands as a weakness that can be taken advantage of by an opponent. That is why Taijiquan requires one to have the whole body working in unison. One must practice tuishou frequently. Tuishou is a practical application and is the only way of accurately testing the form. Learning Taijiquan and its postural requirements is like manufacturing the different parts of an item of machinery. Tuishou is like its assembly. If all the different components of the machinery are made to requirement, then it is easy to assemble the machinery. However, if the parts are wrongly built and are either too big or too small, or if they are simply the wrong parts - it will be impossible to build the machine" (Chen Xiaowang).

Chen Xiaowang further stated: *"one needs to practice tuishou; check on the forms; understand the internal force (jin 劲); and learn how to express the force (fajin 发劲) as well as how to neutralise the force (huajin 化劲). If one is able to withstand confrontational push hands, then it is an indication that one has understood the underlying Taijiquan principles".*

A generation before, Chen Zhaokui 陈昭奎 also advocated that effective Taijiquan tuishou skills are constructed upon a solid groundwork of forms training, stating that *"taolu 套路 is the foundation of tuishou; tuishou is a device for* testing the correctness of taolu. And tuishou is a bridge between the form and free fighting. Doing tuishou without practicing taolu can gain some skill in self-defence, but without the foundation work you cannot improve and raise your skill to a higher level".

It is important to remember the purpose of tuishou practice and not to let competitive egos take over. Speaking of training in Chenjiagou in his younger days Zhu Tiancai, one of the foremost current masters to emerge from the village, said, *"The purpose of tuishou is not competition. The purpose is to learn skill and techniques".*

The chief coach of Chenjiagou Taijiquan School Chen Ziqiang陈自强, 20th generation of the Chen Family lineage wrote, *"Tuishou is not a competition of strength but that of skill. The fulcrum of lever and spiral conversion makes it possible for 'four ounces to deflect a thousand pounds四两拨千斤'. One develops this skill through the use of centrifugal and centripetal forces, with the spine acting as the central axis, so that movements go around an internal circle that despite its relatively slower speed can overtake an external circle".*

Calligraphy in the Chenjiagou Taijiquan Museum: *"Four ounces to deflect a thousand pounds"*.

By the time a practitioner trains tuishou, he would be expected to have a clear understanding of how to use the body in accordance with Taijiquan's strict movement principles. The exercise is built around the exchange of the different methods or energies between the two partners. For instance, when one person utilises pressing (an按), his opponent uses warding (peng掤) to counter. When one squeezes in (ji挤), the other diverts away (lu捋), and so on. Chen Changxing stressed the importance of painstakingly studying the different energy methods in his *"Song of Hitting Hands打手歌"*: *"Be conscientious about peng, lu, ji, an; complementing each other above and below, (it is) difficult for others to advance掤捋挤按需认真, 上下相隋人难进"*. Besides the more obvious manifestation of peng, lu, ji, an, hidden within are a wealth of techniques such as adhere, connect, stick and follow沾 连 粘 随; pluck, split, elbow and bump采 挒 肘 靠; leap, dodge, fold, and empty腾 闪 折 空; grasp, take, throw and strike 抓 拿 摔 打etc.

Developing the *jin* of the body therefore is central to tuishou practice. Essential to accomplishing this is a meticulous study of Taijiquan's Eight Methods or *Bafa*八法. From these eight methods or energies all skills and techniques are generated. Each type of *jin* denotes a specific combat skill or capability that can be expressed through numerous techniques. All are carried out at close range and involve an approach comparable to wrestling techniques except that it is more reliant on rooting, structure, coiling and Chen Taijiquan's explosive power emission. The eight energies are made up of four frontal methods (sizheng四正) that are familiar to the majority of Taijiquan practitioners: warding (peng掤); diverting (lu捋); squeezing (ji挤) and pressing (an按); and the less familiar four diagonal methods (siyu四隅): plucking (cai采); splitting (lie挒); elbowing (zhou肘) and bumping (kao靠). It is essential to be adept in these four skills for a practitioner to attain a proper appreciation of the throwing and striking skills that Chen Taijiquan is renowned for. Unlike the four frontal methods, *cai, lie, zhou* and *kao* are typically instilled when the student begins practicing at higher speeds and with more force (Berwick, 2000).

The Essence of Taijiquan 太極之粹

Chen Taijiquan practitioners should also sought to fulfill the tuishou principles of *"adhere, connect, stick and follow 粘连黏随"*, *"neither lose contact nor resist 不丢不顶"*. These principles are based on observing the requirements of: no excess *(wuguo 无过)*; ability to reach *(nengji 能及)*; follow and yield *(suiqu 随屈)*; extend to accommodate *(jiushen 就伸)*, in accordance with the Taijiquan Treatise that says *"neither excess nor deficient, follow to constrict and extend to contain"*. Whilst teaching tuishou Chen Zhaokui regularly said, *"whoever follows wins the battle"*. Individuals often use force with the arms to deflect a push, or become off-balanced. In both instances they are making the error of not following; in the first case by using resistance *(ding 顶)* to meet an incoming force and in the second case unable to follow and yield. In the process of tuishou, the training partners continually discover and solve contradictions. In this way the ability to *"adhere, connect, stick and follow"* is honed. Then comes the ability to *dongjin 懂劲* (to understand one's own and a partner's energy) and *fangjin 放劲* (to subtly put out or emit the correct amount of force in accordance to a particular situation).

Chen style Taijiquan traditionally has five methods of tuishou, each designed to train different skills:

Wanhua 挽花 - fixed step - single and double-handed
Dingbu 定步 - fixed step - double-handed
Huanbu 换步 - forward/backward stepping - double-handed
Dalu 大捋 - moving step - low stance - double-handed

Luancaihua乱采花 - free steps - double-handed

Beyond these is the practice of free pushing or s*antui* 散推 that is built around a method of upright grappling and joint locking – particularly effective in readying an individual for the realities of combat.

The first method *Wanhua*挽花 *(Rolling Pattern)* is often the introduction to tuishou and commences the training of working with a partner – to train the ability to manage one's posture and energy as well as cooperating with and managing that of a partner's. In this method the student practices the circular patterns of wanhua which involves each person taking turns to lead and follow. It trains the ability to stick to the partner's movements by following and yielding. All movements are in accordance to the principle laid down by the reeling silk exercises. Chen style exponent Wang Haijun who had won numerous tuishou contests advises, *"The first step is to train the body to be pliant and relaxed. Let qi sink down to the dantian and flow correctly. Then train 'listening' or tingjin*听劲 *- listen for the jin of the other person, be aware of where his force is. It requires a sensitivity of the contact point connecting yourself to the other person, and the feeling to follow his energy. In this exercise you don't do any fajin, you just listen and follow and try to develop good contact".* Wang Xian王西安,one of the so-called four Buddha's Warrior of Chen Taijiquan, advocates varying one's speed and stances, so that one starts to train the ability to adapt to different circumstances. The movement requirements present in the *taolu* is maintained in *tuishou* – slow and not broken, quick and not dispersed and fast and not scattered. The shoulder joints must be extended and flexible to enable full rotation. The body moves as a integrated unit, *"not off-side, no leaning, no inclining; always following the guidelines for training".* Through repetitions of this basic exercise, first single-handed method and then the double-handed method, the fundamental requirements of *tuishou* practice is realised and one can move on to the more complex pattern.

The second method is the double-handed *Dingbu*定步 (Fixed-step) which emphasises the training of the four frontal methods/energies *peng, lu, ji* and *an*. Still using the rolling pattern, both partners use no force against each other, and try to identify the *peng,lu,ji,an* within the circular pattern. During this stage both sides alternately shift weight without stepping. All requirements are as above. With diligent practice, one begins to understand

Chenjiagou students demonstrating "Dingbu" – Fixed Step Push Hands

the energy within the pattern, gradually making it more precise and usable. One can also explore the quality and direction of the *jin* of a partner and to follow and yield to incoming force as well as identifying opportunity to advance.

The third method is *Huanbu*换步 *(*Changing-step). This stage introduces stepping into the routine in order to train the synchronisation of the hands, eyes, body and legs and foot work. During training both partners continue to identify the four frontal methods of *peng,lu,ji,an* within the circular pattern. Each circle encompasses a forward and backward step *(jinyi tuiyi*进一退一*)*, using *ji* and *an* on advance and *peng* and *lu* on retreat. Stepping is steady and placing (of the foot) must be precise and balance must be maintained in transition. Also within the drill is the opportunity to learn how to recognise weaknesses in a partner's position. At this stage you are trying to find your partner's weaknesses and mistakes; you don't create confrontational strength against each other but through the following, listening and stepping you try to identify opportunities. To avoid any confrontation against each other in force you learn to neutralize if there is any potential or intention of incoming force". Within this method is the potentials for techniques such as shoulder and elbow strikes, bumping, grasping and throwing, as well as attacks with the legs such as hooking and sweeping. When the drill becomes very familiar and fluid, the numbers of stepping can increase to three steps or five steps, thus bringing more flexibility to the footwork.

Dalu 大捋 (Big Divert) is the fourth *tuishou* of method. This method is a progression built upon the foundation of the previous methods. The movement pattern is similar to the last exercise, but this stage requires both participants taking a much longer and deeper stance, usually with low crouching stances. This demanding exercise trains the individual's *"roots and stamina and the coordination between the roots and waist so you can move up and down and also practice the exertion of power from the crotch and waist"*. It trains leg strength, agility and changeability as well as stability of the lower plane. In this method the four diagonal energies *cai, lei, zhou, kao* are added.

As the student's level of skill improves, they will progress onto the fifth method *Luancaihua* 乱采花 *(Random Pattern)*. The footwork is compact and agile, with spontaneous step patterns which are precise and steady, and which very much depends on the specialism of each person. The hand pattern is the same as before but with rapid changes to accommodate or take advantage of the position of a partner. This method is akin to freestyle push hands and begins the training for free sparring. The practitioner continuously advances with stepping to occupy the space of the partner, and uses manoeuvres such as bridging (*da* 搭), sweeping (*sao* 扫), rolling(*gun* 滚), tying(*shuan* 拴) and so on to subjugate the person without prior notice. Bridging maintains a connection and yet distancing an opponent from one's space; sweeping make it difficult for an opponent to read one's *jin* direction he is being redirected (swept) away from one's centre; and rolling and tying renders it impossible for an opponent to gain access to one's space as his manoeuvres are constantly being rolled away and his posture tied up. In this way the opponent is unable to attack and is completely under one's control.

Chen Xiaoxing and David Gaffney training Huanbu (Changing Steps) Push Hands

After achieving competence in all five *tuishou* methods, practitioners can progress to free sparring based on the foundation of free *tuishou* practice. Now they can begin to practically study the combat potentials of Chen Style Taijiquan. Working at all times to maintain a strong root and to maintain constant limb and body contact, each partner attempts to neutralise the incoming forces of the other and to cause the other to lose balance. At the same time both look to apply their own attacks from the system's extensive arsenal techniques. The whole process of *tuishou* training enables the practitioner to increase not only their sensitivity, but also their reaction time and ability to make the correct judgment immediately an opportunity presents itself. Waiting for the best opening so that a single technique is enough to defeat an opponent.

Chen Taijiquan free sparring

Supplementary Drills for Tuishou

Chen Taijiquan also employs a number of supplementary exercises to complement the push hands drills. For example:

> Two persons performing *kao* (bumping) in order to train timing and distancing. In a drill that emphasises footwork and the precise placement of technique, two persons train bumping with the hips, front of the shoulders and the back of the shoulders.
>
> "Sticking leg" training is used to practice leg locking, pressing and bumping as well as yielding and neutralizing skills. This drill involves two partners connected at the knees following each other's movements in a figure-eight pattern without losing contact or applying force. With practice, this enables a practitioner to unsettle an opponent's stance and structure with minimal movement.
>
> To be able to cope with the high physical demands in *dalu* in terms of leg strength and flexibility, Chen Zhenglei advocates training the cloud hands (*yunshou* 云手) action from a deep horse stance, as well as performing calisthenics such as high repetitions of squats (one hundred times plus) and single-leg squats.
>
> Training with the long pole (*dagan* 大杆) is a traditional method of training the dantian. The long pole can help to bring out the "jin from the dantian" (generating strength from the centre), passing out to the feet and hands. Regular practice can help to make one's dantian strong and power discharge explosive. The drill also trains balance and stability in the lower plane whilst handling a heavy object.

Through the process of strict, accurate and repetitive training the practitioners continually work towards increasing their level of skill until they reach a stage where they can effortlessly read an opponent's intention, while at the same time be in control of their own intention. "This type of push hands method and the theory of understanding *jin* is based on a foundation of traditional martial arts techniques that are then further developed. From the external shape of combat method it is internalised into a discipline whereby *"internal qi is hidden within"* and there is an *"interchanging of the internal jin"*(Gu Luixin, 1998). The Taijiquan Treatise

Chen Wangting created *tuishou* as a way of training fighting skills in a practical and safe way.

stated: *"From familiarisation to gradual realisation and understanding jin; from understanding jin to entering into 'shenming' 神明"*. The idea of *shenming* (of entering into a level that seems to be wondrous and mystifying as actions are instinctive and unpredictable) is often cited as the highest point of Taijiquan achievement. What is referred to is not some quasi-religious state, but rather a level of attainment that is beyond the realm of human understanding and therefore appears superhuman. However the statement continues: *"Without diligence and time, this enlightenment will not be obtained"*

Classical Weapons Training For the Modern Boxer

Most traditional Chinese boxing systems contain a broad arsenal of weapons for conditioning the body as well as training coordination and strategy drills. Classical Chinese martial arts almost universally train with the four primary weapons – doubled-edged straight sword, broadsword/sabre, spear and staff. Besides the classic weapons, Chen Taijiquan makes use of a wide range of long and short weapons, reflecting its roots as a battlefield art. While their importance is obvious within their historical context, people often wondered if they are of any relevance to today's practitioners.

In today's society, most people train Taijiquan for its health benefits and for personal development rather than for life-or-death combat. From this perspective weapons training are viewed by many as an unnecessary anachronism. However, this represents a superficial understanding of the role of weapons training within the overall training curriculum, as each weapon trains and reinforces different aspects of Taijiquan that helps to develop the physique and attributes of the Chen boxer.

Chen Xiaowang demonstrating Double Broadsword

Photo courtesy of Estevam Ribeiro

剑/Jian

Despite being a complex and technically difficult weapon to perform, the **sword** *(Jian 剑)* is usually the first weapon taught. The sword is one of the oldest weapon forms in Chen family Taijiquan. The form incorporates the skills of hands, eyes, body and footwork together with the spiral rotational movement principles of Chen Style Taijiquan. With power and control held in the wrists, the nature of the sword form trains flexibility, agility and speed and also encourages one's postures to be open and expansive. The movements stretch the body's joints and strengthen them, particularly developing strong wrists and hands. In this way one's *jin* can be extended out beyond the extremities into the weapon, thus allowing each core technique to be executed fully and effectively. The form also calls for nimble footwork and wrist control. *Traditionally heavy swords were incorporated into the training regimen of the serious practitioner in order to develop the ability to handle weapons that require considerable physical strength whilst at the same time execute them with pliancy, looseness and dexterity.*

Taijiquan Sword Core Techniques

Stab (Ci 刺) The sword is held horizontally or vertically. Power is transmitted to the tip of sword. The arm and sword forms a straight line.

Chop (Pi 劈) This is a vertical action from the top to the bottom. Power is kept in the body of the sword.

Scoop (Liao 撩) *Liao* is an upward movement with vertical sword. Power is in the front of the sword.

Hang (Gua 挂) In *gua* technique, the sword is held vertically and with the point of the sword leading the power moves downwards from above.

Point (Dian 点) With the sword held vertically flex the wrist so that the tip of the sword points down quickly. Power is in the tip of the sword.

Slice (Mo 抹) Level slice - The sword is held horizontally and goes from the front to the left or right in an arc. Power is in the middle section of the sword.

Block (Jia 架) Held vertically, move the weapon upwards diagonally to above the head to block. Power is in the middle section of the sword.

Sweep (Sao 扫) The sword is held horizontally and goes sideways to the left or right level with the calf. Power is in the middle section of the sword.

Intercept (Jie 揭) The sword moves obliquely to the top or to the bottom to intercept. Power is in the front part of the sword.

Plunge (Zha 扎) The sword is lifted up horizontally with the hand facing outward to plunge down sideways.

Push (Tui 推) The sword is held horizontally at the front of the chest and then push to the left or right with power release.

Neutralise (Hua 化) Any action in the sword form that changes the path or power route of an opponent is known as *hua*.

Davidine Siaw-Voon Sim in *Deity Points the Way* posture.

刀 Dao

The broadsword (Dao 刀) or sabre is another of Chen Family Taijiquan's short weapon. Where the sword form is nimble and lively and often compared to a "saltant dragon 游龙", the character of the broadsword movements is direct and powerful and is likened in Chenjiagou to a "ferocious tiger 猛虎". Movements mainly involve the weapon coiling around the head and wrapping around the body (chantou guonao 缠头裹脑). The form is often performed with long, low stances and powerful leaping movements. Each broadsword technique is enhanced by the appropriate foot placements, footwork, leg methods, leaps and turns. The traditional heavy broadsword (rather than the flimsy modern *wushu* version most widely seen today) makes obvious the conditioning benefits of the sabre form. As there are thirteen core techniques in broadsword, the form is also known as "Thirteen Sabre" (Shisan Dao 十三刀).

Taijiquan Broadsword Core Technique

Chop (Pi 劈) Using the edge of the weapon, go from behind upwards, then forward and downward in a continuous sequence for chopping.

Cut (Kan 砍) Use the edge of the broadsword to cut to the left or right downwards or sideways.

Pierce (Zha 扎) With the arm and weapon forming a straight line, the tip of the broadsword is directed forward for stabbing. Power is sent to the tip of the weapon.

Roll (Gun 滚) The right hand holding the broadsword, the left hand presses down on the spine of the sabre and then push and turn to the left or right.

Coil (Chan 缠) With the right hand holding the broadsword, the right arm rotates inward to lift up with the tip of the weapon pointing down. The spine of the weapon passes the left shoulder, staying close to the back and then passes the right shoulder to sweep towards the left until it reaches the left flank.

Lift up *(Liao 撩)* The edge of the broadsword moves upwards, sending power to the front section of the weapon.

Hang *(Gua 挂)* In *gua* technique, the weapon is held vertically and with the point of the leading the power moves downwards from above to either sides of the body.

Slice *(Mo 抹)* Holding the broadsword horizontally and with the arm straight, draw the weapon back in an arc movement to the left or right side towards the inside of the arm.

Fend *(Jia 架)* With the edge of the weapon facing up, move the broadsword diagonally upwards to fend off. The weapon is held just above the head, and power is focused in the middle section.

Block *(Dang 挡)* With the tip of the sabre lowered, use the edge of the weapon to block an incoming weapon.

Pick *(Tiao 挑)* Use the spine of the sabre to execute an upward lifting movement.

Shake *(Dou 抖)* Stab the broadsword horizontally either to the front or to the side, at the same time taking a step forward. The power of the waist combines with that of the crotch to produce shaking power.

Intercept *(Jie 揭)* With the right hand holding the broadsword, the arm rotates inward for the edge of the weapon to go downwards diagonally to the right side of the body. Power is sent to the upper middle section of the edge of the weapon.

Chen Xiaoxing: The character of the broadsword movement is direct and powerful and in Chenjiagou are likened to a "ferocious tiger".

枪 Qiang

Chen Family Taijiquan traditional training also incorporates a number of long weapons including the spear (qiang枪) and the Spring & Autumn Broadsword 春秋大刀 (also known as the halberd or guandao关刀).

The Chen Family **Spear** (*Qiang* 枪) form incorporates both spear and staff techniques and is more accurately referred to as the Pear Blossom Spear with White Ape Staff (*Lihua Qiang Jia Baiyuan Gun* 梨花枪加白猿棍). In its many variations the spear was an ever-present weapon on the pre-modern Chinese battlefields. The spear form helps in the development of fast and accurate footwork as well as improving upper and lower body co-ordination. It facilitates the transmission of energy from the back through to the shoulders and arms and enhances the synchronisation of the eyes, hands, body and steps. The intricacies and complexities of its form is reflected in the saying *"it takes one hundred days to train the broadsword but one thousand days to train the spear"*. Techniques switch from spear to staff and are obvious in the routine.

The Essence of Taijiquan 太極之粹

Core Techniques of Chen Style Taijiquan Spear

Pierce (Zha 扎) Use the point of the spear to pierce downwards or sideways.

Fence (Lan 栏) To block and intercept with the body of the spear.

Drape (Pi 披) The spear is kept close to the body and coordinates precisely with the footwork.

Burst (Beng 崩) Using whole body integrated power, send the weapon sideways and backwards, energy concentrated on the pole and not the spear head.

Sweep (Sao 扫) In the form the spear is held horizontally and sweeps transversely to the left or right.

Point (Dian 点) Holding the spear towards the end part of the pole, do a small circular movement upwards, sideways and then downwards.

Pick (Tiao 挑) Sliding the hands towards the spear head to reveal the staff end, flick the staff obliquely upwards and forwards. Or using the pole end flick the spear head obliquely upwards and forwards.

Chop (Pi 劈) Using the length of the weapon, wield upwards, then forward and downward in a continuous sequence.

Draw *(Ba 拔)* Extract by pulling the spear back with one hand whilst keeping the other hand in control of the weapon.

Fend (Jia 架) To block and intercept with the middle section of the spear.

Wind (Jiao 绞) Hold the lower end of the pole to wind the spear in a circular motion, making sure the circle is tight and compact.

Spear v Guandao: photo from the Chenjiagou Taijiquan Museum

Coil *(Chan 缠)* Coiling spiralling movements are present in all the techniques used.

Stab *(Ci 刺)* - using the momentum of the body, the tip of the spear is driven forward in a swift movement to stab

春秋大刀 Chunqiu Dadao

The Spring & Autumn Broadsword (*Chunqiu Dadao* 春秋大刀, also known as guandao 关刀) is regarded as Chen Taijiquan's heavy artillery. Unlike the spear and the pole, the spring & autumn broadsword historically was the most often deployed weapon by Chinese military officers. Due to the exclusive and expensive nature of the weapon, it became a symbol of military rank, and was often ornately decorated. The name *guangdao* derived its name from the legendary Chinese general Guan Yu, who was respectfully given the title of Lord Guan (Guangong 关公), from the tumultuous "Three Kingdoms" period of Chinese history. He reputedly used a weapon weighing eighty-two *jin* 斤 (one *jin* is about five hundred grams). This was also the favoured weapon of Taijiquan's creator Chen Wangting. Because of this he acquired the nickname "Equal to Guan Yu 赛关公" because of his military exploits and his proficiency in the use of the *guandao*. The dynamic nature of the *guandao* form, with its sudden changes in direction, sharp turns and explosive leaping movements makes it a wonderful body-conditioning tool. Today's practitioners use weapons ranging from a few kilograms to more than twenty kilograms. Its practice is based on thorough grounding in the core skills of Taijiquan, as it demands a stable lower plane, good upper body strength, and excellent spatial awareness. As with the other weapons, there are thirteen core techniques that are expressed clearly in the form.

Core Techniques of Chen Style Taijiquan Spring & Autumn Broadsword

Chop *(Pi* 劈) To cleave or chop vertically.

Hack (Kan 砍) Downward horizontal movement using the sharp end of the blade.

Lift *(Liao* 撩) An upward slicing movement with the weapon held vertically and power held in the front of the blade.

Hang *(Gua 挂)* The weapon is held vertically and with the point of the blade leading the power moves downwards from above to either sides of the body.

Cut *(Zhan 斩)* Using the edge of the blade to cut downwards or sideways

Slice *(Mo 抹)* Level slicing with the sword held horizontally and goes to the left or right in an arc with power held in the middle section of the blade.

Parry *(Zai 截)* To offload an incoming attack.

Fence *(Lan 栏)* To block and intercept with the middle section of the blade.

Pick *(Tiao 挑)* To lift upwards and forwards obliquely with the end of the blade.

Stab *(Ci 刺)* A straight piercing movement with the tip of the blade.

Push *(Tui 推)* The weapon is held horizontally at the front of the chest and then push to the left or right.

Ward Off (Jia 架) To ward off by raising the weapon overhead.

Pin Down *(Tuo 拖)* To drag the weapon across an opponent's body and pin it down.

Chen Style also trains with the **long pole** (dagan 大杆). The pole is at least three metres in length and is used as a means of increasing whole body power and *fajin* capabilities. The practitioner trains either a pole form that consists of thirteen methods that have been compiled into a sequence, or by training individual movement drills. The seventeenth generation Chen Fake is said to have performed three hundred repetitions of the "pole shaking" exercises. In Chenjiagou both the spear and the long pole are typically made *from a particular kind of wood called bailagan* 白腊杆 *(white wax wood)*, a strong but flexible wood that bends to absorb impact preventing damage to the weapon. As well as form training for whole body strength, a number of two-person "sticking" drills are also practiced to enhance the 'listening' ability and combat skill of practitioners.

David Gaffney and Chen Ziqiang training with the long pole.

The extensive weapons rack at the Chenjiagou Taijiquan Museum

Though rarely seen in the wider world, within Chenjiagou knowledge of a wide assortment of traditional weapons has been preserved up to the present. Some, like the two section pole form, have evolved from agricultural tools to gradually become incorporated into the Chen Family Taijiquan weapons syllabus. Others have been handed straight down from the battlefield. As well as the aforementioned, weapons practiced today include, double swords, double broadswords, double maces, and the 3 and 8 movement pole forms. Maintaining the tradition of training in these classical Chinese weapons enhances an individual's overall skills, preserves an unbroken tradition of martial culture and greatly increases one's physical and cardiovascular fitness.

CHAPTER FIVE

INSIGHTS

Chen Xiaowang 陈小旺 – Preserving a Legacy

Chen Xiaowang was born over sixty years ago in Chenjiagou (Chen Family Village). Today he is the nineteenth generation 'gatekeeper' of Chen Family Taijiquan, and has been designated as a "living treasure" of China. The following is an interview in which he relates his personal Taijiquan journey.

The Early Years

I started Taijiquan from a young age, learning from my father (Chen Zhaoxu 陈照旭) from about the age of seven. Training would usually be in the evening after school. But most evenings I did not feel like training. After mealtime I would lie on my bed to go to sleep but I would be dragged up. It was very much "reactive" rather than "proactive". There was no choice in the matter, for there was always the threat of a beating. At the time, my father taught me Laojia. After the death of my father, when I was about ten, my fifth uncle (Chen Zhaopi 陈照丕) retired and returned home and I started studying with him.

At that time, (Chen) Zhenglei, (Wang) Xian and (Zhu) Tiancai were not in the village yet. Others - Dewang, Wang Dang, Li Qingshen, Li Dingchen – these village people were around then. The last wife of Chen Zhaopi would lead us to practice, while fifth uncle would sit on a chair watching and correcting us on movements he thought were not right. Usually he corrected only one or two movements, or would perhaps adjust one posture. The training was mainly geared towards the older children; I was just tagging along as I was still young and he would not teach me. I "filled the gaps" of the older children, going forward in between their routines to do mine. Fifth uncle thought it was amusing and would give me a few words. He didn't know me and wondered which family I belonged to. That was how I started training from fifth uncle.

A lot of people have wondered why I said I learned from my father and was trained by fifth uncle. What's the difference? From my father I learned only *Laojia Yilu "Kong Jiazi*空架子*"* (the outward shape of the form without knowledge of its content) and memorised a set of movements. The important thing is not whether you've learned a traditional form, but to what level you trained in this form. I learned everything else from fifth uncle, including weapons and the different methods of push hands.

Like I mentioned before, in the beginning I didn't have any interest in learning martial arts. However, by the time my father taught me, my interest was aroused. When I was between eight to ten years old, Chen Lizi came back from Xian. He was the same age as my father and weighed over 90 kilograms, as did most of his brothers who were known for their big size. They had built a new house. The outer beam was between two and three metres tall. Some people had arrived from a district east of the village to locate their linage for inclusion in the clan book (This happens when a clan member had left the village many generations ago, and was now unable to locate the point of linage – A process would be set in motion where the village heads would try to trace their ancestors from the time of Chen Bu and then reinsert their names in the clan book). My father being an active member of the village had been invited for this occasion which took place in Chen Lizi's house.

An early picture of Chen Xiaowang

Chen Lizi was very strong and had trained to quite a good level of skill. But he had not yet achieved the level of "*zou hua* 走化" (the ability to absorb and neutralise). My father entered the door and as he shook hands with someone, Chen Lizi, in an attempt to test my father's skill, took his arms from behind in a seemingly unbreakable reverse joint lock. My father executed a technique which threw Lizi three metres high feet first, head down which would definitely have killed him if he landed on the ground.

Chen Boxian and Chen Lizi's mother Chen Liyeh witnessed this; in all there were around 10 people in the room. Chen Boxian told this story many times. I wasn't present as I was still young. Chen Lizi himself also related this incident. The manner he was thrown head down was really precarious and he would certainly have sustained fatal injuries if my father hadn't dashed forward and caught him with his arms and knee. This story about my father's skill was widely circulated in the whole village and inspired me to want to practice and train more. I practiced consistently up to the time fifth uncle arrived back at the village. He continued my development and trained me in Laojia, Paocui, Sword, Sabre etc. Zhenglei came to the village at some point and Tiancai and Xian also joined us about the same time.

Preserving the Family Legacy

The family name was a big factor. My grandfather's name is well respected. I remember when I was thirteen or fourteen years old, I was on a bus on a rare occasion when I went to a place ten kilometres away. I was still small in stature and children didn't travel very often. People on the bus asked me where I was from, I said Chenjiagou. They asked if I knew Chen Fake. I said Chen Fake was my grandfather whereupon everyone on the bus stood up to look at me. That incident had a big impact on my development, as I was made acutely aware of my legacy and my responsibility towards it, and that this legacy should not end with my generation. That motivated me to train hard and well from the traditional and practical angle.

At that time I trained very hard – intense concentrated training. At the same time our diet was very poor. My clothes would invariably be soaked through and even in the winter my woollen coat would be saturated with sweat. To what level of hardness? If I couldn't move my legs to get up I would feel so happy. I never complained or slacked and this was completely driven by interest, there was no thought of monetary benefit. And then there's work. At that time it was farming and the work was hard, with little spare time. After that I learned carpentry, where I thought the work would be lighter and leave me with more energy for practice. But carpentry turned out to be hard work! So I decided to incorporate training into work. Shaving wood would be like fajin (one pushes forward with the whole body) integrating the strength of the whole body. Whatever you do you don't deviate from the movement principle. At that time the family status was deemed problematic and for a day's work I only earned two jiao. That was not unusual. Sometimes not even two jiao. However food was provided and that was good food.

My motivation at that point was legacy. I started out of interest and then realised my responsibility. In my family, every generation has produced famous and skilled individuals and I felt that that couldn't stop with my generation. But aspiration is just that – aspiration. You can see people who have great aspirations and start to practice very hard but after a while they lose the drive. Also life is not consistent. You cannot plan to live to one hundred years old. People who were the same age as me – Chunlei, Xushen, Zongfu – they've been dead some years now. I have to think at the time: "do I do this or do I concern myself with making money?" Once you've thought this through then you have a clear goal. I realised one thing, "*mo shi zai ren, chen shi zai tian* 谋事在人，成是在天" for example, whatever you plan to do in life, whether you succeed or not, if during the process you become ill or die, this is beyond your control. You have to set your heart on doing something and then try your utmost to achieve it. And if it doesn't succeed, you would have done your best – it won't be because of lack of effort. When I realised this saying it became the tenet of my life.

So it goes on – train and train. Push hands, *nafa* 拿法 (seizing method), all required painstaking and serious training. My main training partner was Dewang 德旺 who was seven or eight years older than me. (Let me think, at that time Zhenglei was not at home, Tiancai was an occasional partner). Dewang was very strong. My way of thinking was, when you trained with friends you should train as if you're going into battle, then when you go out you'll have no problem. If you are afraid of this person and that, or if you're worried about your own weakness, that's the area you should train, and try to turn the weakness to strength. I was between sixteen to eighteen years old then and was still small in size. In fact I was small until about twenty. My push-hands was definitely inferior and I couldn't beat Dewang who was twenty-seven or twenty-eight and was fully-grown. I was often

Middle row second from the left Chen Zhoukui. Far right Chen Zhaopi. Front row right – left Chen Xiaowang, Zhu Tiancai and Chen Xiaoxing.

hungry as well, but we always pushed for several hours. I was flung to the ground countless times, but always picked myself up and advanced forwards again. My body got bigger eventually.

One day we decided to practice qinna and I put on a really good technique. He laughed and I laughed. We were very innocent then and didn't bear ulterior motives or bad thoughts. This was the first time I got him and he was also very pleased "you've improved" he said. He trained so very hard but from 1970 onwards stopped Taijiquan altogether.

In 1964 my young uncle (Chen Zhaokui 陈照奎) came back for the first time, and I learned Xinjia from him. He also taught me *nafa* (After he left, I practiced this but was still not familiar with the usage of the techniques. So I looked for the techniques through the *shenfa* 身法 *(body mechanics)* of Xinjia. From 1965 – 1967 uncle came home several more times. I learnt

Xinjia Yilu, Erlu and Qinna from young uncle. Training has to be disciplined. Sometimes after work you'd just put your head down for a little rest and wouldn't wake till morning, so I'd just sit and rest and then practice.

Life began to improve by 1974. The most important change was that we had enough to eat and were not constantly hungry. As for training and how often, my stipulation to myself was that it should be consistent and progressive. I would permit no excuses, like not having enough time, too much to do, having visitors etc. If I set a target of twenty repetitions, then whatever the circumstances, even nineteen would not do. I wouldn't go over and do twenty-one either. If that were absolutely not possible, then whatever I miss today would be added onto tomorrow's practice. One time both my feet swelled up as a result of an infection and I was unable to put my feet down and weight-bear with them. I still trained my usual reps with my feet off the ground. I'm fortunate that I didn't fall ill. I may get the odd cold, but that's all.

Sporting Elite

After the dark years of the Cultural Revolution and following Mao Zedong's death, there was a revival of martial arts and it was seen again as something worth preserving in the country. In 1980 I was selected by the Henan Sports Council to go to the Zhengzhou Sports Academy to be hothoused alongside other elite participants from other sporting fields, such as basketball, volleyball etc. All we had to do was train in our own chosen fields. These were specially selected people who were there to take part in competitions. [Chen Xiaowang won gold medals three times from 1980 to 1982 in National Martial Arts and Taijiquan Competition and was elected as the chairman of Henan Province Chen Style Taijiquan Association in 1984].

From then on, the food I ate took a big change for the better. Normally people would spend twenty to thirty yuan a month, but our allocation was about three hundred to three hundred and fifty yuan a month. Also there

1979 National Wushu Exhibition Henan Province team. Back row Chen Xiaowang and Zhu Tiancai (Taijiquan). Front external martial arts reps.

was a specially employed cook to prepare all our meals. We had so much to eat that there was always surplus. Everyday there were about twenty dishes to choose from and there was milk, honey, soya milk and soup. We ate really well. When I was at home with no facilities I was training hard, how could I not train even harder?

I stayed there for ten years, but the very intensive training lasted for two years. I did very hard and focused training. At one point a friend of mine Ciao Bao, who was on leave at the time, said he wanted to train with me. I agreed and everyday he trained with me for three hours following me through my routine. I just did my own training doing the usual reps I do with no compromise. After a week he was so exhausted that when he lay on his bed he had difficulty getting out. He had difficulty moving his arms and his muscles were aching so much he could hardly dress and undress and turn over in bed. It shows the intensity of the training. I was doing a lot of new techniques that involved very intensive physical training. At that time I was very motivated throughout. No matter how physically demanding the training was, I always coped with it.

The intensive training only stopped after I was transferred to the Wushu Centre and I gradually had to take on more official duties. It would have been good if I were able to train for the whole of the ten years. In 1990 I went overseas.

Taking Taiji Overseas

When I first arrived abroad, I experienced language barrier, lifestyle change and isolation, as I had no family… but these did not daunt me. My biggest challenge was my fear that the foreigners would not be able to understand Taijiquan and consequently would not accept it. In order to popularise Taijiquan, the first task must be for the public to accept Taijiquan. Through trials and errors and studying different methods of demonstration of the form, I hope people will know the true face of Taijiquan. I hope that in this way people will understand Taijiquan, develop an interest, and then participate. It was in Australia that I planned the spread of Chen Family Taijiquan, which has come to fruition now. In each place I visit, I support and coach the facilitator, so that he or she is able to promote Taijiquan in that particular area. It is not possible for one person to do everything. It's the method of duplication that has led to the expansion of Chen Family Taijiquan.

I have travelled all over the world in my wish for Taijiquan to be transmitted to as many people as possible. Sometimes the travelling is tiring but I feel joy in my heart to see how people have embraced the art. One is only tired when one is forced to do something one doesn't like. However, as more people take up Taijiquan, the weight of responsibility increases for those who transmit the art. The responsibility to transmit the authentic art and to enable people to understand the true principles of Taijiquan. This is my legacy.

The Essence of Taijiquan 太極之粹

Chen Xiaowang

Chen Xiaoxing陈小星: Understanding the Taolu

The Principle of the Chenjiagou Taijiquan School, Chen Xiaoxing is a nineteenth generation master of Chen Family Taijiquan. The following pages contain a number of discussions with Chen Xiaoxing about the various handforms in the Chen Taijiquan curriculum and their unique features. He also describes his own "Taijiquan Journey" and his thoughts on the situation of Taijiquan today.

Q: The Taolu of Chen Family Taijiquan consists of two main frames today: The Old and New (*Laojia 老架* and *Xinjia 新架*, respectively), each consisting of a First Routine 一路 and Second Routine 二路). Can you elaborate on the evolution of the Old and New frames?

CXX: Chen style Taijiquan was created by Chen Wangting (1600-1680) in the ninth generation of the Chen family. The original art was made up of five boxing routines that were handed down for five generations until the time of Chen Changxing (1771-1853). He synthesised the routines practiced at the time into what is known today as the Old Frame First Routine (Laojia Yilu) and Second Routine (Laojia Erlu), also known as the Paocui 炮捶 (Cannon Fist), that together make up the foundation forms from which subsequent generations of Chen Village practitioners have developed their capabilities until the present day.

The overriding principle of Taijiquan is the co-ordination of soft and hard and of fast and slow movements. The characteristic of the first routine leans more towards soft and slow. With this basis one would practice until the body's posture is correct; until the shape and qi are harmonized and one can physically manifest this understanding; not simply intellectually theorising it. The next progression would be the Cannon Fist, the aim of which is to train and increase stamina and explosive power (*baofali爆发力*). With the two sets together you then fulfil the requirements of "*gang rou xiang ji 刚柔向济*" (mutual existence of hardness and softness).

The next significant evolution within Chen Family Taijiquan is the development of the New Frame. The routines devised by Chen Changxing

The Essence of Taijiquan 太極之粹

Chen Xiaoxing

continued uninterrupted until the seventeenth generation and my grandfather Chen Fake. He went to Beijing in 1928 to teach Taijiquan. During the decades he was in Beijing, based on his own understanding, experience and knowledge, he added new movements onto the Old Frame, still adhering to the principle of Taijiquan, to create the New Frame branch of Chen family boxing, which is widely practiced today.

The handform provides the foundation upon which all the other skills of Taijiquan are subsequently built. Whether you are following the Old or New Frame, the most important thing is to give one hundred percent mentally and physically. Factors such as patience, persistence, *yi* (mind intent), strength, relaxation, and qi are fundamental in increasing one's Taijiquan skills.

Q: Why do you think Chen Fake create the New Frame?

CXX: In essence the Old Frame and New Frame are the same. In contrast, however, the New Frame has more explosive movements and therefore is more demanding physically. In this sense, the New Frame is considered more suitable for people who are younger and fitter. Many of the Beijing people who initially went to Chen Fake had already practiced martial arts to quite a good level and were eager to see the applications hidden within the original routine. So he added extra movements and manifested more outward expression with more obvious martial functions. The main difference is that there is more changing of *jin* 勁 (trained focused power) and more short *jin* within the New Frame.

Q: What are the Unique Characteristics of the New Frame?
CXX: The Old and New Frames should not be viewed as different entities because both are foundation forms. If you look beyond the superficial differences, the Old Frame and New Frame are the same style, sharing the same origin and guiding principles. However, the latter is harder to perform well because of the complexity of the smaller spirals, and so the former is usually taught first. In Chenjiagou, the Old Frame is used as the foundation form because it is steady and fluid, so it is easier to understand and to realise the principle.

The main characteristics of the New Frame are the smaller circles, the extra emphasis placed upon the turning of the wrists and the more visible folding of the chest and waist. Rotations of the waist and dantian are also more obvious. The New Frame additionally lays greater stress upon bringing out the spiral energy usage in applications, with extra *fajin*发劲 (power release) and *qinna*擒拿 (joint locking) movements throughout. The form also consists of more dynamic, springing and leaping movements. If you really want to strictly separate and compare the two, the smaller spirals of the New Frame are harder to execute and the internal feeling of the form takes longer to experience. If incorrectly understood, this often leads to erratic, exaggerated swaying movements, which can look very ugly.

However the fundamental principles of the two frames are the same with regards to postural requirements and movement principles. Both require the practitioner to exhibit movements that are continuous, round and pliant, connecting all movements section by section and closely synchronising the actions of the upper and lower body. Irrespective of whether one practices the Old or New Frame, it is consistency that will eventually bring results. Repetitive practice of the form leads to complete familiarity with the movements. Over the course of time co-ordination and flexibility are naturally attained throughout every movement.

Q: Is it true that Chen Fake created Xinjia, but Chen Zhoukui standardised the form?

This is a common misconception. To be precise, Chen Zhaokui is the one who spread and popularised the New Frame. After the death of his father in 1957, he travelled extensively in the 1960s teaching in Shanghai, Nanjing, Zhengzhou and other cities. In the 1970s he came back to Chenjiagou every year. So it would be more accurate to say that the New Frame was created by my grandfather, but was taught by my uncle.

Confusion has arisen because of the wide variation in how the New Frame is performed even though it is a relatively new form. Chen Fake's students stayed with him at varying periods of his life and for different lengths of time. The new form took a period of time to evolve and some students came during his early days in Beijing, some later. Most of them practiced for a period and then left. Chen Zhaokui is the only one who was with him from beginning to end. That is why if you look throughout China you can see different interpretations of Chen Fake's teaching.

For example, practitioners in Shandong Province mostly follow Hong Junsheng's 洪筠生 style. In Beijing, different groups can be seen practicing in the styles of Chen Zhaokui 陈照奎, Feng Zhiqiang 冯志强, Lei Muni 雷慕尼 and Tien Xiuchen 田秀臣 among others. The various interpretations should not come as any great surprise. Everybody has got his or her own unique body shape, size and temperament. Just as I'm teaching the few of you here, each individual within the group has a different physique and practices according to his or her own level of understanding - and all go away and say they have learned from Chen Xiaoxing.

Q: Why do we need to practice Paocui?

CXX: The key distinguishing feature of the *Yilu* routine is the use of *rou* or softness as the core quality. The *Paocui* form in contrast incorporates hardness as the most important principle. Taijiquan is constructed upon the theory of *gang* and *rou* balancing as well as alternating with each other.

As a result, with the two routines there is a comprehensive balanced system co-ordinating hardness and softness. Paocui is characterised by fighting techniques expressing many *fajin*, swift movements, sweeps, elbow and shoulder techniques and unexpected changes of attack and defence. The form is physically very demanding and a strong foundation of skill in the Yilu is essential if a practitioner is to benefit from the Cannon Fist routine. People are often too anxious to learn the Paocui before they have learned to do the Yilu well.

Before practicing the second routine all movements must be refined, and all stiff, clumsy and uneven actions eliminated. You have to practice *Yilu* well before you practice *Erlu*. *Paocui* is trained to develop your *baofali* (explosive release of strength) and *naili* (endurance and stamina). The two must go together. When you are doing the explosive movements it is no good if you are panting and out of breath. *Paocui* is easy to learn, but difficult to train. Easy in that if you already have the foundation of Yilu, there are many repeated movements. Also the form is much shorter in length. However, the difficulty level of the form is higher and the exercise intensity is greater. Performed with greater speed, more *faijin* and many leaping and stamping movements, it provides a demanding workout that rapidly increases the practitioner's martial strength.

In this context we can understand the logic behind Chen Family Taijiquan's traditional emphasis upon Yilu as a foundation for the Paocui. Slow practice enables the practitioner to be aware of details; to ensure that postures are accurate; to check stability and balance throughout movements; to augment lower body strength; to co-ordinate internal and external actions; and to realize the circulation of *qi* throughout the body. All these are not possible if one performs the movements rapidly at the beginning and energy is dispersed each time a movement is performed forcefully. As one's level of skill improves, movements should be a combination of slow and fast, without any loss of detail. At this stage the practitioner is ready to begin training the Paocui.

A distinctive feature of the Paocui is the speed. It is faster, the practitioner being required to perform it rapidly, but without the form being scattered or dispersed. You should maintain your movement requirements without losing the *chansijin*. Although the movements are fast, you still need the fast and slow alternating rhythm.

The form can also be characterised by the frequent employment of *fajin* by a variety of different parts of the body. Alongside the fist, elbow, shoulder, knee and foot used in the external martial arts, Chen Family Taijiquan requires the practitioner to be proficient in releasing power with whichever part of the body comes into contact with an opponent. You must be able to issue energy, whether it is a throw, strike or *qinna* (joint-locking) movement, without any pre-warning to an opponent. When issuing power, the movement must be spontaneous and natural. Forcing the movement increases the stiffness and resistance held within the body. Speed and power can be substantially amplified by lessening the level of energy lost en route to the end point. Any tension within the muscle (or joints that have not been fully opened) will provide resistive forces that pull the striking area back. This causes energy to be released through the trajectory of the motion, lessening the amount of energy getting through to the end point.

A common mistake is to over-emphasise the use of force when performing paocui. Following the principle of yin and yang, Taijiquan combines the hard and soft energies smoothly and interchangeably regardless of whether one is practicing the *Yilu* or *Paocui*. Not only can any part of the body *fajin*, but strength can be changed internally, blending attack into defence and vice versa. The key to efficiently releasing power lies in relaxing the body and mind and utilising the waist.

During the explosive movements of the Paocui, the ultimate aim is to harness one hundred percent of the body's strength. To accomplish this the energy is generated from the feet through the legs to the waist, where it is intensified by the spiral movement, then joined with the energy produced in the arm and fist. *Jin* or internal strength must start from both feet. Failing to apply a movement from a firmly rooted position denies that movement a source of power. Resistance from the floor allows energy to

go through the body sectionally to form a complete integrated system. Without the rebounding energy from the ground, powerful whole-body strength is difficult to achieve.

The explosive nature of the Paocui is nowhere more apparent than in the frequent leaping and jumping movements. During these, it is vital that you maintain both a feeling of lightness and heaviness. For example, when your hand and leg go up during a movement, your centre of gravity (zhongxin 中心) should be sinking down. Otherwise the movement will be floating and without substance. You must understand the reason why you are doing the jumping or stamping in order for the movement to be concentrated and focused and for the whole body strength to be coordinated.

Q: Is the use of intrinsic energies (*peng, lu, ji, an* etc) the same during the Paocui?

CXX: While all Taijiquan forms follow the same underlying principles, the expression of *bafa*八法 (eight essential energies) within the Pao Cui is not the same as the Yilu. The Yilu uses *Peng, Lu, Ji* and *An* 掤捋挤按 as the mainstay of the routine, supported by *Cai, Lie, Zhou* and *Kou*. The essence of Paocui is not the same; the form predominantly expresses the energies of *Cai, Lie, Zhou* and *Kou* 采挒肘靠, this time supported by *Peng, Lu, Ji* and *An*. Throughout both forms the *jinlu* 劲路 or route of energy is also different. Although both use rounded arc movement based upon *chansijin* (silk reeling) movement, the Paocui movements are slightly straighter. Even though the route is still spiral and round, the circle is smaller and the speed is faster.

It is important of being aware of the implications behind the alternating of fast and slow movements. For instance, during *fajin* as the *jin* finishes, the *yi* or intention continues. After each explosive movement is completed this serves to connect the *jin* to the next movement. Before releasing force, energy must be stored by allowing the *qi* to sink and collect fully in the *dantian*. Releasing energy before this point will result in a movement powered largely by the upper body. Immediately relaxing after an explosive movement causes the body to recoil, collecting the energy in readiness for the next movement.

The form must be trained until it becomes continuous, with each movement flowing naturally into the next. The speed should be fast, but controlled and contained. The breath must be co-ordinated with movements and should not be laboured and the *jin* should employ whole body strength.

Q: How different is the Taijiquan teaching in Chenjiagou to that outside?

CXX: When you go outside to teach seminars etc., you only get to teach a few hours each day with a long break in between seminars, whereas in Chenjiagou there is a continuous input. Also you are living within the environment of Taijiquan.

The teachers who go out to teach, no matter how good they are, are only teaching for a short period of time, so it is more difficult to teach in details. If a movement is incorrect – in Chenjiagou a teacher would ask you to repeat, repeat, repeat. For example, just do *Jingang Daodui*金刚捣碓 today. Realistically it is not possible to do this if there are only a few days available.

Teaching depends a lot upon understanding how to teach, the environment and the mood of both the teacher and student. Because it is not just learning, but looking and watching as well. When you are in the environment, everywhere you turn you can see people training. This provides important role models for students and serves to motivate their practice.

Q. *What was your Taijiquan path?*

CXX: Everybody's development is characterised by stages. In the beginning it was very much a passive, externally driven process. Pressure to learn came from everywhere - family, family name, family legacy, parents, siblings and so on. When I reached ten years of age, I didn't have a lot of

understanding. When my fifth uncle (Chen Zhaopi陈照丕) was teaching I understood a little bit. Chen Zhaopi never scolded anybody - his teaching way was not to scold anybody into learning. It's up to yourself. I remember that he used to say *"when you learn Taiji skill, if you choose to learn it and not use it, it's up to you and it's not that crucial. But if you learnt it but are not able to use it- then that is very important. Then as far as martial arts go, you've learnt nothing"*.

After I'd grown up and started working and began hearing more about my family, I realised that I did not want to be the one to spoil the family name. When I was younger my practice was sporadic and not consistent; at times when I was not in the mood or lazy I would slacken in my practice, but when I was in the right frame of mind, I would train and practice like a demon. There were times when I practiced harder than anyone else. My practice became consistent when I began to work outside the village. When people realised that I was from Chenjiagou, they would automatically presume that I was of high skill. At that time I decided that I was going to train properly and not be on and off in my efforts.

Did you learn mainly from Chen Zhaopi?

CXX: I was very young when Chen Zhaopi was teaching, but I was always around and liked to listen to his explanations and stories. I remember the teaching of Chen Zhaopi very clearly but by the time I knew how to train properly, he was gone and my brother Chen Xiaowang did most of the teaching. Really, every youngster, when very young, all they learn is the form and movement. In their minds they don't have any plan or method of what to do with the practice. For me it was the same. From Chen Zhaopi and Chen Zhaokui it was just a matter of following on with no clear intention in my mind. I subsequently did a lot of training with my second brother Chen Xiaowang.

Q. Chenjiagou itself is undergoing changes very rapidly - how do you think it will affect the development of Taijiquan?

CXX: Progress is such; it always goes forwards and not backwards. I don't think that it will adversely affect Taijiquan. As conditions improve it will only attract more people to come in to learn it. As people's living standards improve, they start to think more about the quality of life. If all your preoccupation is with making enough money to fill your stomach, then you really don't have the energy or time to pursue other things. It's only when you don't have to worry about food and clothing at a subsistence level, that you can start to think about the quality of your health and body and how to improve your life. This is why, during the time of great hardship, Taijiquan was almost abandoned - before Chen Zhaopi came back (and revived it).

Q: Now in the West, more and more people are learning Chen style. What are your feelings on the spread of Taijiquan in the West?

CXX: Taijiquan, from the time of its creation to now, has undergone a sea change. From the time Chen Changxing taught it to Yang Luchan, an outsider, the system has opened up to the outside world. In the past, it was considered a family system, now it is open to all. Anyone who has the interest to learn has the opportunity to learn. It doesn't matter what country, race or colour they have. There are two main stumbling blocks: The barrier of language and subsequent communication difficulties; also the understanding of tradition and culture that is incorporated in Taijiquan's philosophy. Things that are taken for granted in the Chinese language are non-existent in the western language. Consequently the learning process takes longer. It is impossible to close that gulf immediately. You have to go through a gradual slow process, but you will get there.

Q. In the past, the teacher-student relationship was different than the one today. Before people didn't pay, but today it is conducted like a commercial exchange - what is your opinion?

CXX: That view is completely wrong. In the past they did take payment, but the payment method was different. Nowadays, the student comes and negotiates with the teacher and says how much for an hour - and that hour is given to the person. In the past, the teacher only taught when he felt like it, there was no fixed time. People assume that in the past no payment was required. This is not logical. Take for instance, my uncle [Chen Zhaokui 陈照奎] as he travelled around China teaching. If he did not get payment, how could he have survived? In the past, the payment was often in kind, sometimes a student would help in the house, or do work for the teacher. In my grandfather's [Chen Fake] time, there was one student who worked in a medicine shop - he didn't pay for tuition but whenever anyone in the family was sick, he would bring medicine without charging.

Also there was a tradition of the rich paying, but the poor not – so, in effect, the richer would subsidise the learning of the poorer ones who wish to learn but have no money. The children from the village who come to learn at my school today do not have to pay.

Q: Teachers always emphasise training concentrated *jin* and training the Taiji body, but most people say they have limited time to practice. What do you think is the best way to practice?

CXX: Whether you practice the Old Frame or New Frame routines it is more important to know how to approach the learning process. Gongfu 功夫 (fundamental skill) is really about time. It is only from lengthy practice that you realise the skill. It is like going to school, it has to be progressive. You have to spend one year in primary one, another in primary two and so on. You cannot spend half a year in primary one and expect to go to primary two and then jump to secondary school, university etc. You have to put in the time. The most important thing is to pay attention to the teacher when he is teaching you and then practice according to the teaching during whatever time you have.

Unfortunately, that is the route you have to take, there are no two ways about it. People somehow think that in the past the teachers had a lot of time to practice and didn't have to work like people do today. Actually, work nowadays is much easier, with people usually having a set time of maybe eight hours a day. When we were doing farm work, we didn't have machines. Even when machines began to be used to ease physical labour we could not afford to buy them. Work was very hard and not limited to a few hours a day.

Really, it just requires discipline and organization. If you work an eight-hour day and want to spend two hours of your day on training it is not impossible. You can easily fit ten repetitions of the form in two hours. Do this every day and in 365 days, imagine how many repetitions you will have done. It is all a matter of determination and perseverance. It is all about your mindset, if you really want it.

The Essence of Taijiquan太極之粹

Chen Xiaoxing: "It is all a matter of determination and perseverance. It is all about your mindset, if you really want it".

An early shot of Zhu Tiancai taken in Chenjiagou in 1981

Zhu Tiancai 朱天才 on Chen Taijiquan's *Fajin*

"Fajin must be performed as though "shaking cinders from the back of the hand" or like "a golden lion tossing its mane"".

- Chen Family Saying

A distinguishing feature of Chen Taijiquan is the recurrent use of explosive powerful movements or *fajin* 发劲. Along with the fist, elbow, shoulder and knee used in the external martial arts, Chen Taijiquan requires the practitioner to be able to *fajin* with whichever part of the body that comes into contact with an adversary. This can be utilised to throw or strike an opponent. Alongside sensitivity, yielding and redirecting skills, a practitioner seeking martial efficiency must be capable of powerful aggressive movement.

The following notes on Chen Taijiquan's *fajin* were collated during Zhu Tiancai's visit to England in 2002 to teach, for the first time, the 42 methods of *fajin* that he has developed, based on the 32 *fajin* pattern created by 18th generation master Chen Zhaokui. In the course of Zhu's teaching he gave a number of characteristics about the method of issuing energy in Chen Style Taijiquan:

There should be no deviation from the core principles of Taijiquan - relaxation, whole body movement etc. Execution of any *fajin* arises from a particular point within a circle, so the silk-reeling spiral path of a movement should always be sought. The waist is the primary, central axis and is the base from which all movement begins *(以腰为主宰)*. When executing fajin the primary training principles still hold i.e. using your waist as the axis, the body should be interconnected and aligned in such a way that when one part of the body moves every part of the body moves in tandem *(一动全动)*. Ensure that alignment of the upper body and lower body is not broken, and strive to complete the *fajin* movement in one single, continuous flow without breaking your intention or your qi.

The practice of *fajin* should only be done after one has acquired the pliant energy (*rou jin* 柔劲) of Taijiquan. *Fajin* should be done within the principle of '*song* 松' (letting loose or maximum relaxation of the muscles and joints – Zhu Tiancai repeatedly emphasised the idea of attaining forcefulness and power from softness): *"The whole body should be song. Qi sinks down to the dantian* 丹田*, descends into the yongquan* 涌泉*, and then surges into the four limbs. The springy elastic force of fajin is expressed in the outer section of the limb, driven by the middle section, which in turn is activated by the root section"*

When executing *fajin* one should seek to harmonise internal and external movements; co-ordinate the actions of the outer shape and internal energy; clearly differentiate weight distribution; and pay strict attention to timing. The ultimate aim is to harness one hundred percent of the body's strength with precise body structure and alignment during a movement. Therefore, power emitted should be complete, the speed must be quick, the range should be short and the end point must be precise. Clearly differentiate weight distribution. Qi follows *yi*意), and *xing*型 (structure) follows t qi. Therefore, *yi*, qi and *xing* become one entity.

(While Chen Style Taijiquan makes use of rapid turning movement of the waist and hips during *fajin*, this aspect is often over-emphasised. Shaking the body without having a fixed point of impact may appear impressive visually, but is of little practical use against an opponent).

Reverse abdominal breathing is a prerequisite of correct practice. In performing *fajin*, the practitioner should inhale when gathering and exhale when executing. The abdomen contracts during inhalation and distends during exhalation. Above all, breathing should be natural and spontaneous. If the breath is forced, then it is unnatural and detrimental to health (reversed breathing is used unconsciously whenever a person makes a sudden violent effort, even if they are completely unaware of it. Just as a person could not breathe in when pushing a car or lifting a heavy object, one cannot inhale when performing *fajin*).

Fajin is more than simply emitting brute strength. Rather, it is a sudden explosion of power whose quality is relaxed, fluid, springy and pliant that is devoid of stiffness. Though many people perceive Taijiquan as a slow motion dance-like exercise, one's thoughts must go back to the reality that it was created as a martial art. Tales of past masters reveal many references of superior strength and power alongside great softness and sensitivity. *Fajin* training is important in so much as the ultimate objective of Taijiquan practice is to reach a state of balance, fifty percent hard and fifty percent soft, yin and yang balance.

[Zhu Tiancai explained that Chen Zhaokui devised the thirty-two pattern of *fajin* for the purpose of an exhibition in 1975 to demonstrate the dynamism of Chen Style Taijiquan. Chosen to perform was the then very young four Buddha's Warriors of today, Chen Xiaowang, Zhu Tiancai, Wang Xian, and Chen Zhenglei, together with their senior martial brother Chen Dewang. The occasion was the Xinxiang Wushu Tournament, where many renowned old masters were invited to demonstrate their skill, notably Chen Yuxia (daughter of Chen Fake), Lei Muni, and Feng Zhiqiang. In the process of the repertoire, the five members moved in sequence, making square, rectangle and plum blossom (five-ring) patterns on the stage. All who saw the demonstration were impressed by the vigour and energy of the display.]

The Essence of Taijiquan太極之粹

The explosive power of Zhu Tiancai

The *fajin* methods reveal the martial applications and intent contained within the handforms of Chen Style Taijiquan. Zhu Tiancai in recent years recompiled the *fajin* pattern and added ten movements to the original thirty-two so that a comprehensive compendium of *fajin* possibilities can be demonstrated. While the forty-two methods can be practiced as a continuous series, Zhu Tiancai suggested they could most effectively be trained as single-movement exercises. Dismantling the pattern and drilling the fajin methods individually will greatly develop the ability to use them practically. Taking out difficult movements, such as *Ying Men Kao*迎门靠(Open and Bump) where the chest is used as the striking area, or *Wai Bai Li Shuai* 外摆里摔 (Outward Swing and Inward Throw) and practicing them repeatedly can greatly help the practitioner to enhance their accuracy, speed and timing. Chen Zhaokui stressed the importance of single posture training as a means of enhancing martial skills that could not be practiced safely with a partner, saying *"some applications of the movement cannot be used in push hands. For example elbow strikes… and also attacking vital points of an opponent, or qinna"*.

The Essence of Taijiquan 太極之粹

Chen Ziqiang: The Four Essential Elements of Martial Skill

Twentieth generation Chen descendant Chen Zhiqiang 陈自强 is the eldest son of Chen Xiaoxing 陈小星. He is responsible for the day-to-day running of the main Taijiquan School in Chenjiagou. In the following pages he compares traditional and modern approaches to Taijiquan training:

For me learning martial arts was a very natural thing to do because Chen Taijiquan is a family art. Because it is a family art handed down over many generations, it was simply not an option not to do it. Also because I am the eldest in the family, they were very strict with me. I started learning Taiji even before starting school, from about three or four years of age. Every day after school my father made me practice. In time it becomes like a ritual. Every day I know when it comes a certain time; if I don't practice someone will come and tell me off. Consequently, the training habit was formed naturally from a young age.

In the early stages, therefore, training was not really proactive, but reactive. I was compelled to do it. As a child I was very active, so at first I didn't really like Taijiquan, because it is very slow. I liked the very obvious kicking and punching movements. However, the requirement at that stage was to practice every day. It is like building a house, we need to lay down a proper foundation first.

In time I became self-motivated as I came to realise that the content of Taiji was very rich, containing many hidden qualities. Taijiquan is like any other martial art, when you reach a certain level you discover the intricacies and the complexities within the discipline. From around sixteen or seventeen years old, my interest deepened and I no longer needed my father to be after me to practice.

Today my main job is the day-to-day training within the school. In fact, I am in charge of every aspect of the instructional side of the school, particularly training for competition and also the school syllabus – what the pupils need to learn, time allocation, how to teach it etc. As far as each individual is concerned, I base it on three factors, firstly the persons constitution, second their interest and third the time available.

Some people come to the school for a longer period of time, with the hope of achieving some competition results – their training regime will be different to reflect this. Some are there to make their body stronger, for general fitness – so their training requirement would not be so rigorous. Some people have a weak constitution, but are quite flexible and can stretch into a nice posture so we would gear them towards form competition, demonstration and performance. The very strong ones will go for the combative side. In the school students are not just lumped together and taught collectively, rather each student's requirements are considered individually.

When somebody registers, what can be achieved depends on the length of time they stay at the school. If just for a short time, then they are put in the general class and practice *taolu* 套路 (handform). For the ones who are at the school for the longer term, the first month will be like an assessment

Chen Ziqiang: "For the students in the school today, training is of necessity a combination of traditional and modern methods".

period, they learn *taolu* – while we watch their attitude and aptitude. If he is of the right material, we may start thinking towards the tuishou 推手 and *sanshou* 散手 route. Failing that, we gear them towards the demonstration and exhibition. Failing those two, leave them in the *taolu* class and let them develop slowly building foundation.

Long-term would be over three years. Anything less is considered short-term. In Taijiquan, if you haven't got two or three years, it is difficult to reach any level of meaningful skill. It needs that very basic period of time to be able to grasp the basic *gongfu* 功夫 (trained skill) in order to be able to progress further. [Two or three years might not sound long, but the students in the school begin training at six in the morning and are still training when darkness falls! The best of them stay on to become instructors in the school].

Taolu is the basic training method for everybody. Having said that, for youngsters it can get very monotonous. You have to keep their interest and motivation levels high, so sometimes I mix in other stuff to lighten up the training – *taolu* is the foundation, but you can't ask them to just do this day in day out. The main thing is that they have to be stimulated and happy and want to be there.

Rootedness and Structural Integration

The most important thing to look for in Taijiquan training is *"what is beneath your feet"*. The saying is "if you train *quan* and don't train *gong*, the end result is empty" *(lien quan bu lien gong dao toh yi chang kong*练拳不练功，到头一场空*)*. This saying is applicable to all *wushu*武术 *(martial arts)* disciplines. If you look at two old people: one can't stand and can't sit, just lying in bed, no *gong* in his legs; the other stand up very firmly with strength in his legs – people would say he has good *gongfu*.

Di pan 低盘 (lower plane) is representative of Taijiquan as a whole. *Di pan* is like a big tree with deep roots, that won't get blown over by a strong wind. Consider the tree - from its outward appearance it looks very balanced and doesn't look as though it is going to topple or lean. Leaves are abundant and all together it gives off a feeling of balance and strength. In training we look for this same quality – you have to get this strength and balance. [Taijiquan's *"xiapan gong* 下盘功*"* entails the cultivation of lower body strength. Using the feet as the base, legs as support, with the *dang*档 (crotch) rounded, flexible - naturally sunken and stable]. The most important thing is to have *tong yi*统一, which means literally *"whole body oneness"*. This refers to the integration of structure and co-ordination, with the whole body taken into account rather than separating the different parts of the body. The Taiji saying is that *"everything moves together to give oneness in co-ordination and oneness in structure"*.

For the students in the school today, training is of necessity a combination of traditional and modern methods. Now youngsters are required to go in competition at seventeen or eighteen years of age. To get results they have to have more specific training to make up for immaturity of age.

The Essence of Taijiquan 太極之粹

Chen Ziqiang: "Everything moves together to give oneness in co-ordination and oneness in structure".

The Four Essentials of Combat Skill

In most combat or competition encounters an individual is traditionally said to depend on four key factors:

gongfu 功夫 (trained skill)
jishu 技术 (knowledge of technique)
suzhi 素质 (body constitution)
li liang 力量 (physical strength)

It is not possible to fast-track *gongfu* or fluency with a broad range of techniques. These aspects are only possible with time and experience. However, it is possible to fast-track physical strength and body conditioning. As far as the student's at the school are concerned, a high level of *gongfu* is obviously out as their age is young and they haven't acquired it yet. Technique is also so-so because they have not been trained for long enough to be familiar with a wide range of techniques that can be brought out at will.

Traditional Taijiquan training develops the twenty-four groups of muscles in the body in a slow methodical way. Nowadays people train differently; bearing in mind that most students are not going to be in the village for as long as I have been, I look for ways to accelerate the training process. The student's constitution or physical state can be worked on and their strength can be increased. Strength can be trained with weights etc and the physical state can be trained everyday through running, jumping and climbing drills. These two aspects can be developed in a short time.

The strength training method is highly specialised. You are not training to develop *"stupid strength"* (localised strength that is not functional). This is training strength in the waist. Your hand strength is like the hook you use when you are towing a car. You have to remember that your hand is the hook. Your strength is coming from the waist and how you push into the ground. Combining the strength of the car and the rope. The hook is only the implement that connects the two. So when you lift the big rock, it is the strength of the legs and waist and not the hand.

[Author's note - Strength training is not a new phenomenon in Taijiquan. In the past, it represented one aspect of an all-encompassing training process. In Chenjiagou, within the garden where Chen Changxin is said to have taught Yang Luchan, founder of Yang style Taijiquan, can still be found an eighty kilogram stone weight that they are said to have regularly trained with. Traditional strength training methods such as pole shaking and practicing with heavy weapons continue to be used up until today. Over the centuries strength, endurance, and agility have been physical attributes highly valued within Chinese military circles. Military training has utilised activities such as weight lifting, long distance running, jumping, climbing, and swimming alongside the development of martial arts prowess. General Qi Jiguang's training manuals, inspirational in Chen Wangting's creation of Taijiquan, outlined a comprehensive training regimen which included: *"maintaining an overall strong fighting constitution (through remaining "lean and mean"); strong hands and arms through training with heaver than normal weapons; strong feet and legs through running over 600 yards without gasping for breath, using ankle weights (bags of sand) while running; and overall bodily strength and endurance by training while weighted down with heavier than normal armour"* (Henning, 1995).]

It is very rare to find someone who has achieved excellence in all four aspects of gongfu, technique, constitution and strength. In my family so far, for example, since Taijiquan was created it is said that only Chen Wangting, Chen Changxin and Chen Fake have achieved this. The rest of us are striving to be as close as we can to this perfection.

For my students, at their age – in combat the training has to be from slow to fast. At the beginning, the basic thing is to work on their ability to assess timing and distance. The most important thing in combat is to know what constitutes a safe distance from your opponent. First the student must be able to assess the reach of an opponent's arms and legs. Secondly, at the precise moment that an opponent comes forward, that is the point to attack. This can only be executed through experience. Timing and distancing cannot be taught except by going into the situation. The more experience you have, the "wiser" you become.

Sanda 散打 is one of the basic aspects of wushu. The *sanda* we do at the school incorporates the Taijiquan principle, especially the neutralising skill. We also explore the *tuifa* 腿法 (leg methods) of Taijiquan. There is a misconception that there is no *tuifa* in Taijiquan, but this is a mistake. It is just that many people do not know how to use, or overlook the Taijiquan *tuifa*. In terms of *shoufa* 手法 (hand methods), like all *gongfu*, you get the palm, hook and fist. Taijiquan is the same – it is only when in usage, it is not so obvious. Now I am letting the team out onto the *sanshou* circuit to gain some experience, while exploring how to get the most from these methods.

The Future of Taijiquan

Many people nowadays begin practicing Taijiquan with the simple goal of increasing their level of health and fitness. As long as you are training Taijiquan you are improving your body, which straight away makes you stronger than the person who doesn't do it. Therefore, as soon as your body is fit you are able to defend yourself. As far as serious practitioners are concerned, human nature is such that the more you get the more you want. The more people practice, the more interest increases as people study what each move is about. Therefore interest will only get more and more, rather than less and less.

The future of Taijiquan is bound to change, especially the evolution of Taijiquan. But my family Taijiquan will not change too greatly. No matter how much the outside Taijiquan changes, the family Taijiquan will not change. We do not want it to change. The only thing we need to bear in mind is to embrace scientific explanations to unlock a very old philosophy. You have to use modern language to explain the art. You cannot shroud it in ancient philosophy and language. The old Chinese Taijiquan philosophy should match with modern scientific language so people accept the discipline for what it is. This is important. If people try to explain it without the backing of the old philosophy it doesn't work either. The two should match up for its survival and continuity.

Wang Haijun demonstrating peng jin

Wang Haijun 王海军 on the Bafa of Taijiquan

Bafa 八法 – the eight methods - of training the body's intrinsic energies/strength (*jin* 劲) provide the foundation of all the skills and techniques of Taijiquan. Wang Haijun, a senior disciple of Chen Zhenglei and three times China National Gold Medallist in Forms, Weapons and Push Hands, emphasised that the correct practice of Taijiquan must be built upon a clear understanding and identification of these energies.

Q: Is it correct to describe push-hands as the mutual exploration of Taijiquan's internal energies?

WHJ: Push-hands acts as an examination of your Taijiquan, to assess whether you are *song* 松 (loose, pliant and heavy) or not and whether your *dang* 裆 (crotch) and *yao* 腰 (waist) are moving properly. It is like a magnifying glass that serves to amplify all of your faults. If the dang and yao are not used properly then your push hands will be stiff and uncomfortable and your spiral movement will not be lively and agile. At this level a person's movement would be stiff and clumsy when trying to use their strength (execute their *jin*). This stiffness is because of the individual's inability to *song* (let loose) and as a result they are unable to release jin to the required place. Two people, through the practice of push hands must reach a stage where they are able to discern the skill level of each other as soon as they touch hands. They should know instantly whether their partner is using whole body *jin* to rotate his body and whether his *jinli* 劲力 (energy strength) is heavy and weighty。

Q: How do the different *jin* relate to each other?

WHJ: When *an* 按 (pressing down) or *lu* 捋 (diverting) are used, the waist and *kua* are utilised to escape it. Pushing hands should be the continuous neutralizing of each other's energy. This is why it is important to understand the *jin* of Taijiquan, so that you know what your opponent is applying and what you should use to neutralise it.

If you don't understand *peng, lu, ji, an* 掤捋挤按, then as soon as you touch hands these are manifested as collapsed *jin* and at every step you will be at a disadvantageous position. This is why you must first identify and practice these jin through practicing the *taolu* (form).

Q: What are the main characteristics of the eight fundamental jin of Taijiquan?

WHJ: The eight fundamental jin of Taijiquan are *peng*掤, *lu*捋, *ji*挤, *an*按, *cai*采, *lie*挒, *zhou* 肘, *kao*靠.

*Peng*掤 is based on many years of Taijiquan foundation practice, most importantly the handform, until you have cultivated internal energy (*neijin* 內勁). *Peng jin* manifests itself as a physical sensation of inward to outward expansion and strength. *Peng jin* within Taijiquan is when you have reached the equilibrium of neither resisting nor falling short.

Of all Taijiquan *jin*, peng is considered the foremost. All of Taijiquan's eight primary energies contain the principle of *peng*. Consequently it is always mentioned first in any discussion of internal energy. Whilst there is much talk about *peng*, a person cannot simply execute it just because he wills it. It requires external posture training combined with internal *jin* training to be able to correctly express it. If you do not have *peng* then you do not have Taijiquan's *jin* and it follows that you also will not have *lu*, *ji* or *an* etc.

The second type of internal energy is *lu* 捋. The main function of this *jin* is to "lead into emptiness" (*yin jin luo kong* 引進落空). *Lu* can be executed in any direction depending on the route of an opponent's incoming force. It can be used as a *"leading in"* movement in preparation for a follow up attack, or as a direct attack technique in its own right. This *jin* is comparatively short, drawing someone into your space. On the receiving end, the person experiences a feeling of panic and "emptiness". This emptiness is not just your thought/intention (*xin* 心) becoming blank. It is like going downstairs in the dark and missing a step. Suddenly your base is gone and the mind becomes void – this is the result you want to achieve when you apply *lu*.

To deflect your opponent's incoming force with *lu* it is important that it is not just expressed in the hands. Rather there must be co-ordination between the torso and the energy of the *dang* and *yao*. Also it is not just manifested in the body, but with co-ordination of whole body spiral and reeling energy with the *lu* movement of the hands.

Ji 擠 is performed in a sequential movement from the feet to the hands. The meaning of this energy is often misunderstood. *Ji*. like *kao* 靠, involves compressing with the shoulders, but unlike *kao*, it does not use

Ji (squeeze) jin

explosive force or *fali*发力 to go forward. Instead in execution the shoulder rotates forward in a gradual rolling movement, generated from the back. Again it should be co-ordinated with the *dang* and *yao* and the reeling and spiralling of the body. *Ji* is generated from the waist to the back and from the back to the arm. When in contact, the aim of this gradual rolling movement is to unsettle the balance of your opponent. *Ji* is very subtle and is a short *jin*.

*An*按 is an energy that is directed downwards in a pressing movement. This requires you to direct your *jin* to your hands and then press down. There should be a clear sensation of downward pressure. In an actual situation, upon intercepting an opponent's incoming force, *an* is utilised by closing one's own energy and at the point of the opponent losing his balance, press down using the heel of the palm. In form practice, *an* is expressed by completely sealing the *jin* in your palm and ensuring that there is no loss of strength as the movement is executed, for example in the movement Six Sealing and Four Closing (*Liu Feng Si Bi*六封四闭).

Cai 采 (plucking) is a combination of rotating, pressing and closing downwards. This type of *jin* is often used when locking someone's forearm. To elaborate, it is applying *lu* with the left side and *an* with the right, or vice versa. *Cai* is combined with weighing down using a rolling movement of your forearm.

In the form any movement that is applying oblique or diagonal force is *lie* 挒 (split). *Lie* is applying force to either side of your own body and also to either side of your opponent's body. Within push hands you can either use *lie* as a forerunner to a second technique, with the purpose of "leading to emptiness", or as an attack in its own right. In Chenjiagou a push hands formula is taught that says: *"when the force comes in sideways you intercept it straight on, when it approaches straight on, intercept sideways"* (*heng lai shu ji, shu lai heng ji* 横来树击, 树来横击). In practice, this energy is often applied by using, for example, your left leg to control your opponent's right leg and then using both hands to attack on one side of his body.

There are many different methods of using *zhou* 肘 (elbow strike). The point of the elbow is used for piercing and penetrating attacks and the flat of the elbow or upper forearm is for level striking. *Zhou* as a close range attack movement is useful when fighting at a range where your hands are ineffective. There is a Taijiquan saying "when you are far don't use your elbow, when you are near don't use your fist" (*yuan bu yung zhou, jin bu yung quan* 远不用肘, 近不用拳) . There are many practical elbow techniques including the 'piercing elbow to the heart '(*chuan xin zhou* 穿心肘), 'elbow to the face' (*ying mien zhou* 迎面肘) as well as various attacks techniques that involve elbowing the soft areas at the side of the body.

The eighth jin is *kao* 靠 (bumping). There are a number of different types of *kao*, for instance *ying men kao* 迎门靠 (open up and bump) and *bei zhe kao* 背折靠 (fold the back and bump). The former is usually executed when you have opened up both arms of an opponent – as in the White Crane Spreads its Wings (*Bai He Liang Chi* 白鹤亮翅) movement in the form. Once an opponent's arms are opened up , this is usually followed with a

Wang Haijun demonstrating kao jin

step forward so you can enter his space. This stepping in is necessary as the *kao* is a close range technique. It is essential to synchronize the action of the *kao* and footwork. If the footwork is not co-ordinated, you cannot effectively use your shoulder. If your step cannot catch up with your body, *kao* will not be effective.

You must not lean too far forwards to reach the opponent when using *kao*. What you must do is lead in the person's *jin* and then your step must go beyond him. Usually you have to step into his *dang* space then you can use *kao* effectively. If the person is a little bit far away, you should not use *kao*. Over-reaching will only have the effect of causing you to lose your own balance.

Q: How important is form training for developing Taijiquan's essential body requirements?

WHJ: Most important of all is ridding the body of stiffness and replacing it with pliability. The form has a lot of complex movement like the turning and folding actions. Through repeated practice you develop good co-ordination of movement and wholesomeness. If you practice a lot, your body will loosen (*fangsong* 放松) and you will achieve an internal feeling of fullness.

The form also involves training and developing your mind intention (*yi nian* 意念): If you don't practice the form you will not have this kind of training – intention, spiral etc. So it will be impossible to achieve the Taijiquan requirement of softness, and you will not be able to get relaxed and soft *jin* (*song rou jin* 松柔劲) as you try to use the different energies.

Q: Can you explain the Taijiquan saying that through softness you ultimately achieve hardness?

WHJ: Based on the foundation of softness you get rid of your stiff and clumsy strength. When you reach the stage where your body is completely loose and pliable, then all movements will be light and agile. This is vital if the different *jin* are to be expressed fluidly and naturally when required. When there is no more stiffness within your joints and they are pliable and loose, then when you are emitting force (*fali*) the joints won't absorb your strength enroute. For example, if your shoulders are very stiff, when you try to punch out to send power to your fist where it is intended, the shoulder will absorb a lot of the strength before it gets to the fist.

With one shake, strength can reach the hand – this can only be achieved by lots of practice of the form, which eventually allows this sequential, unimpeded transference of energy.

The kind of strength, movement and energy that are developed in Taijiquan are difficult to explain in words and must be experienced through long practice to make possible a deep body understanding. When this foundation work is done the root becomes strong, the internal energy becomes full and all other forms become easy and simple to execute.

Tian Jingmiao

Tian Jingmiao 田京苗 – A woman's perspective

Tian Jingmiao is a member of the Beijing Chen Style Taijiquan Research Centre. In the following interview she describes what it was like being the only female disciple to learn from Lei Muni, a famous student of Chen Fake. She also offers some words of advice on the correct approach needed to make a success of Taijiquan practice and for women studying Chen style Taijiquan.

The Essence of Taijiquan 太極之粹

Q: How did you begin practicing Taijiquan?

TJM: "When I was young, my health was not good. The doctors told my parents that if my poor health continues, I would die young. I was diagnosed as suffering from a rheumatic heart problem when I was 8 years old and my condition steadily worsened as I reached my teens. It was when I was in secondary school that I decided to take control of my own life and try any approach to give myself a chance. That was when I thought I would try out Taijiquan. The doctor had told me that my illness is chronic and I would have to find a way of adapting my life to it.

I looked at a few ways that I could make myself stronger. Any kind of exercise that required exertion was out of the question, and having seen the slow and gentle Taijiquan, I decided to give that a try. I visited the park to observe various activities. The outcome was quite amazing. In the first two years, (I went to the park everyday to train) I gradually got fitter, had less medical emergencies and required less and less hospital treatment. My initial contact was with Yang Style Taijiquan".

Q: How did you meet your teacher Lei Muni?

TJM: "After practicing for a further three years, my health continued to improve. At this point I felt great, and felt that I wanted to build on my fitness and do something more energetic and challenging. So I went to Lei Muni *laoshi* 雷慕尼老师 (teacher). I had in fact seen him before, but my health didn't allow me to do his style of Taijiquan. Now five years on I felt I was able to cope with it.

I approach Lei *laoshi* and asked him whether I could learn Chen Style Taijiquan with him. That was in 1976. I told him that I had a weak constitution, due to years of ill health. All his students were fit and strong young men. He didn't have a single female student. I had advice from the sport council teachers that Lei Muni was a good practitioner who had won many accolades. I also saw Tian Xiuchen 田秀臣 (another famous student of Chen Fake] and others. There were many Chen stylists in Beijing at that time.

Tian Jingmiao with her teacher Lei Muni

When I first approached him, he showed some reluctance, having some reservations in case I suffered a relapse with the more physically demanding system. We agreed on a trial period. For a month, I did only *jibengong* 基本功 (basic foundation work) and no *taolu* 套路 (form). He must have seen that I was keen, as I didn't miss a single day, even on a day a bad a sand storm blew up. He agreed to let me continue, and I begun proper lessons with him".

Q: What was the teaching style of Lei Laoshi?

TJM: "Lei *laoshi's* method was meticulous. He would teach me one movement and I would practice this for three to five days. He then reviewed the movement and would only teach me another movement if he were satisfied with my accuracy. In this way teaching was slow. At the end of a section, he would review the section, and unless he's satisfied, I did not get to learn another new movement.

When I finished learning the whole sequence of *yilu* 一路 movements, then followed the period of meticulous studying and exploring of the sequence. In Chinese we say '*zhao* 找 - 'to search'. To learn the movements of a *taolu* is easy, but to do it well and to do it right is not easy; it usually takes three to five years. For me, it took five years to 'get' *yilu* from beginning to end.

In the first year, because I didn't know how to regulate my breathing and didn't know how to *fangsong* 放松 (to loosen up), I was always tired after doing the form, and needed to rest. The teacher said that I wasn't regulating my breaths properly and in parts not loosening up enough.

Previously when I learnt Yang Style, because the movement is gentler and devoid of *fajin* 发劲, normal breathing was sufficient to co-ordinate with the movements. In Chen style, if you don't know how to regulate your breathing when doing the faster and more explosive movements, it leaves you drained and exhausted after one repetition of the form. An inexperienced person would let all the breath out in *fajin* and then need to take in a full breath in the next movement. This makes a person very tired afterwards.

My teacher told me that I should not let out all my breath from the dantian when doing *fajin*. I should only let out part of the breath and then connect with the next intake of breath and in so doing I would be combining natural breathing with *fajin* breathing, and so would not feel any discomfort throughout. This is important for the body's health. Breathing should never be laboured. Also how to regulate breathing to coordinate with each movement, eg. the breath in between each change of movement etc. I studied this aspect for a full year, and also a full year on *panjiazi* 盘架子 (examine the body structure)".

Q: What do you mean by panjiazi?

TJM: "It involved going down on low stances; breaking down and studying every move and every posture; how to fajin, how to connect movement after *fajin*, how to connect movement when there is no *fajin* etc.

In this way five years passed, and Lei *laoshi* said that I was now not too bad. I concentrated on improving my skill and stayed with Lei laoshi until he passed away in 1986".

Q: What was the training attitude in your time?

TJM: We made sure we arrived well before the teacher, to make sure little tasks are done before he arrived. Like sweeping the training area, hanging up the pennant and so on. So when teacher arrived, he could start teaching without distractions. There was a thirst for knowledge. Whenever the teacher explained a point to whichever person, I would go and listen. It didn't matter if I had encountered it before, there may be something I had missed, or had not enough understanding then to realise the message. Or I may be seeing the same thing from another angle. Practice is a matter of repetition, the more you do the better you get.

It is easy to understand a concept, as most students are adults. But to do is not easy, especially in Chen Style Taijiquan. If you understand it intellectually and are then able to do the movement correctly, then it means you have '*wu* 悟' (grasp) the concept. You have no '*wu*' if you cannot do this. Therefore '*wuxing* 悟性' is often spoken about and is very important in assessing a student's ability to progress. '*Wuxing*' cannot be instilled into a person, or given to a person. Sometimes it takes painstaking investigation and rumination to 'see the light'. Once you've achieved this, everything becomes crystal clear, and whenever a teacher demonstrates a point, you could 'see' it straightaway and be able to replicate it. This process is unavoidable, challenging and requires a period of time.

However, some people either haven't got this innate ability, or their learning method is not correct. It may be that a person does not pay proper attention to what the teacher is saying. Every time you let the opportunity to learn slip by, you're losing the chance to progress. I believe you should listen whenever the teacher instructs, whether it is directed at you or someone else.

Q: Do you think the attitude towards training has changed? Why do you think this is?

TJM: In the past, there was definitely more respect for the teacher. And the teacher was able to be strict and demanding with students. Nowadays learners do as they please. They turn up when they feel like it, they may put in effort one day and not at all the next day. They are not disposed to be guided by the teacher. Some learners have a lot of potential physically and intellectually, but they have no staying power. There is nothing a teacher can do about that. People don't see Taijiquan as a priority any more. Sometimes it is pressure from the family. People feel the need to make money.

It also depends on how you perceive Taijiquan. From my own point of view, Taijiquan was a chance for me to regain my health. So for me I consider it to be my best investment. Good health is the best asset one can have. To have a healthy body is better than having a hefty bank account. What good is money if you haven't the good health to enjoy it? This is my personal testimony. I remember the time when I was rushed to the hospital for emergency treatment when my heart failed, when I couldn't breathe. When they revived me, my thought was 'I'm still alive', followed by 'I don't want to die' and 'please don't let me die.' In order to live, I have to rely on myself to find whatever method to make this possible. In the three decades since, I've not had a relapse of the heart problem.

I believe that Taijiquan is very good for correcting chronic conditions if one persists and perseveres. Nobody believes or suspects I have a heart condition now. Bearing in mind that my heart was so enlarged that it was pressing on my left lung. Today I still have the scar tissues of my illness, but otherwise there are no other ill effects. My heartbeat is normal, as most people with my condition have a resting pulse of over 100 (normal around 70-72 beats per minute).

When I do more energetic workout, I observe the requirements of Taijiquan: tongue touching the roof of the mouth, regulate the breaths, adjust the body so that circulation is unimpeded etc. This has helped me greatly. I don't feel tired and I maintain my stamina.

Q: Is there any advice that is specifically for women Taijiquan players?

TJM: I feel that it is more difficult for a woman to reach a high level of Taijiquan attainment. I speak for Chinese women here. This is due mainly to social and cultural reasons. Most Chinese women are expected to take care of family affairs. There is the inevitable break with Taijiquan after they get married. This comes with family responsibilities, usually beginning with pregnancies. That involves at least one year's break from training. Until the child starts nursery, it is impossible for a woman to be committed to come to the park every day. These are the unavoidable facts of life for a woman.

Q: Can a woman practice Taijiquan during pregnancy?

TJM: A woman is advised to avoid any form of vigorous activity during pregnancy. *Taolu* can be done taking a higher stance and posture that is not too wide. The form should be done in the soft relaxed manner and *fajin* should be avoided. Gentle exercise is good for the health of mother and baby. Quiet sitting meditation is good to calm the mood. However, as pregnancy advances, it may affect the balance of the person. Taijiquan is about finding the centre to maintain the correct posture. Pregnancy often throws this askew and awareness and great care must be taken at this stage.

Q: What about during menstruation?

TJM: I personally have not let that stop my practice. It is true that sometimes women feel uncomfortable and less energised at this time. The body retains fluid during this time, especially in the abdominal region. Some women get very bad cramps in the abdomen. How I see it, the symptoms are there whether you do Taijiquan or not, so it shouldn't stop

The Essence of Taijiquan 太極之粹

you from doing it. You can reduce the physicality of the exercise, by not going down too low. In fact, Taijiquan is known to reduce abdominal cramps, regulate the periods, as well as delaying the menopause. Delaying the menopause makes a woman keep at bay the ageing process. People sometimes limit themselves by placing themselves into age categories imposed by social conditioning. When you are at a certain age, you should behave in a way befitting that category. I believe you should just carry on without putting these types of constrains on yourself. Go on regardless and let things develop naturally.

Taijiquan philosophy is the same. The human form returns to its natural state and within this natural state one seeks the principle: What is the principle and why is this principle necessary? What happens when I follow it and what happens when I don't? You gradually assimilate this and acceptance only comes about only with the existence of a principle. This is also true to life. Everything you do needs a purpose and structure. Taijiquan's philosophy is very helpful when applied to our daily life, for example, in our association with other people, and in how we deal with life in general.

Q: What is your concluding thought?

TJM: I am committed to continue the teaching of Lei *laoshi* and the promotion of Chen Style Taijiquan. Lei *laoshi* had put a lot of effort on me, and for that I would not abandon him. From his lineage I'm the only one still teaching. I think of him often, and wish to pass on his lineage through training a new batch of instructors.

This task has weighed heavily on me. To find someone who has determination and perseverance, and has the ability to learn as well as teach. In the present environment of economic growth and rapid change, people's focus is now different. Taijiquan is not a priority in their lives.

For me my morning Taijiquan practice is like my morning breakfast. I need to do Taijiquan just as I need to eat breakfast. No matter what I do, time has to be put aside for this. In my mind, everything has to take second place to my Taijiquan.

The Essence of Taijiquan 太極之粹

Taijiquan: Ancient Art or New Age Fad?

In an interview with BBC Radio's Eastern Horizon, Chen Zhenglei 陈正雷 spoke of the approach needed to take Taijiquan forward into the twenty-first century:

"The biggest setback for Taijiquan and all martial arts was during the Cultural Revolution when people were not able to practice freely and martial arts became outlawed. Taijiquan and other martial arts diminished in China. When China opened its gates again to the rest of the world, its rich culture was promoted and martial arts became standardised and simplified in the process. This had its pros and cons; allowing more people to learn,

but ultimately diluted and changed the virtues of the traditional form.
There is lots of imitation Taijiquan out there, and the public do not know the difference. These eclectic styles will be passed on as authentic and there will be fewer traditionalists amongst Taijiquan practitioners.

The philosophy of Taijiquan is profound, deserving of a lifetime of research and study. Because this philosophy was formulated in an age when there was insufficient scientific knowledge to clearly explain its subtleties, some training methods and theory were explained in an abstract numinous style so that future generations can absorb and understand it in the context of their own era. However, this can easily lead to misinterpretation and mystification of the theories, especially among modern-day Taijiquan enthusiasts, and with beginners. For example, what is *"Taiji neigong*太极内功*?"* How do you explain *"dantian rotation"*? Many people practice a lifetime of Taijiquan but are still unable to resolve these questions.

Through prolonged practice and training, when the body's joints are loosened, the tendons are stretched and elongated, when all parts of the body are co-ordinated in motion, and every gap between the joints has developed elasticity – this elasticity, the stretching of the tendon added to whole body co-ordination is what is known as *Taiji neigong* (Taiji internal skill).

Traditional Taijiquan practice involves what is known as dantian rotation. As far as dantian rotation is concerned, it is simply a requirement for a person to focus on the dantian region during practice. The dantian, according to the study of *jingluo*经络 (main and collateral channels) , is situated in the lower abdomen approximately three fingers below the navel. In this area there is a concentration of internal organs, mainly the reproductive and excretory organs. Concentrating one's mind intent on the dantian region has several benefits: it can lower the body's centre of gravity making the lower plane (*xiapan* 下盘) very steady and balanced; it enables massage of the internal organs to increase the functions of those organs; It can focus the mind-intent (*yinian*意念) so that when you are practicing your quan you are actually resting your mind; to enable the execution of dantian breathing, namely abdominal breathing which increases lung capacity. So dantian rotation is a practice requirement of Taijiquan and is nothing mysterious. Where is the dantian? In your abdomen, besides your internal organs, there is not such an organ. However, if you use an abstract explanation you can say that it is created by long practice. People with high skill have a distinctive feeling as if there is a sphere in the abdomen that is turning when you are playing Taijiquan.

Long-standing practice of Taijiquan enables the *jingluo* to be open and free of obstruction, thereby increasing the circulation of blood. Internal martial artists call this *neiqi* 內气. *Neiqi* can undeniably improve the health. Many old martial texts advocated that the use of qi in attacking an opponent render one indestructible, endowed with techniques capable of penetrating anything. If taken literally it becomes supernatural, entering the realm of myth. Whether it is described as *neiqi* or *neigong* 內功, as long as a method is executed perfectly then it is not magical. In actual martial application one requires technique. This technique is acquired only through long-term training of the body so that reactions are sensitive and reflexive. To achieve this there must be a perfect co-ordination of the mind and body and recognition of the precise moment of opportunity. Amongst other attributes, this requires speed, alertness, positional awareness and the execution of the appropriate technique. For example: in *shuai-fa* 摔法 (throwing techniques) it is necessary to know where all the leverage points are and how you can change them; during *nafa* 拿法 (grasping method) it is necessary to know the anatomical position of all the reversible joints, fulcrum theory and understanding of the dimension and movement boundary of each joint; in the case of *dafa* 打法 (hitting method) one must have an understanding of timing and distancing.

Chinese culture is steeped in allegory and religious beliefs that cannot be explained in practical terms. This gives some people the opportunity to exploit and perpetuate a condition by using myth to explain a superstition or superstition to explain a myth. If people are not mindful they can easily be led down an incorrect tangent. In the last twenty years Taijiquan development and teaching has intentionally or unintentionally been influenced and affected by this phenomena. Using ambiguity to explain something that is quite practical is detrimental to the art. A lot of people who are propagating this mystical thing are actually quite genuine in their beliefs. What is worse are those who use this to exploit the many sincere people who are striving to seek the truth.

Traditional Taijiquan studies have many abstract writings. How do you sort it out in your mind? If the texts cannot be explained in practical terms, if you cannot use them to elevate your Taijiquan skill, then they are of little use. In order to be able to understand Taijiquan you must be able to objectively study it. In the research of this ancient philosophy one needs to adopt modern scientific theory. For example, using the science of the body, the science of movement, using psychology (study of the mind), science of nature etc to explain what appears to be shrouded in mystery. Using the study of fulcrums and spiral movement to explain, for example, the saying *"using four ounces to deflect a thousand pounds"*. In this way one can get away from the fanciful supernatural interpretations. Get rid of the distractions and go for the main point.

18th Generation Chen Family Taijiquan teacher Chen Zhaokui 陈照奎 stood out as a teacher who was able to explain Taijiquan using the language of the body to explain the philosophy of Taijiquan. The unique teaching method of Chen Zhaokui was that he could very clearly and understandably explain the requirement of every part of the body for every movement. This was considered a big leap forward at the time.

The theory of Taijiquan is as deep and as wide as an ocean. For a beginner who has just entered the door it is inevitably extremely difficult to understand. In the process of learning a frame, the beginning student must gradually master the movement principle. To understand one or two points is considered not bad, as it is not possible to understand every aspect at once. Improvement occurs in a step-by-step manner over time. For example, a requirement of all basic movements is that the two outer extremities section (hands and feet) hold the energy, the two middle sections (elbows and knees) hold the position and the two root sections (shoulders and kua) relax. To do all of this simultaneously is very difficult so it is better perhaps to concentrate on one point at a time.

The Essence of Taijiquan 太極之粹

Taijiquan has been practiced for over three hundred years since its creation and is showing no signs of waning. In fact it is going from strength to strength. For its continuing acceptance it has to walk into the twenty-first century, using twenty first century understanding to decipher what is a very ancient philosophy".

Bibliography

Berwick, S.J., The *Five Stages of Chen Taiji Combat Training* in Ultimate Guide to Tai Chi: The Best of Inside Kung Fu, Contemporary Books (2000).

Chen Bing, *Chenjiagou Taijiquan GB interview* in Chenjiagou, 2005.

Chen Xiaowang – *Zhonghua Wushu* magazine

Chen Xiaowang: *Chen Family Taijiquan of China*. Henan People's Publishing, 2004.

Chen Xiaowang: *Chen Style Taijiquan Transmitted Through Generations*. People's Sports Publishing Beijing, 1990.

Chen Kesen. Chen Zhaopi *Henan Sports Journal "Henan Tivu Bao" on April 22, 1993*.

Chen Zhiqiang, *Chenjiagou Taijiquan GB interview* in Chenjiagou, 2003.

Chen Xiaoxing, *Chenjiagou Taijiquan GB interview* in Chenjiagou, 2004.

Chen Zhenglei, Chinatown The Magazine Issue 8, 2003.

Chen Zhenglei. *Chenjiagou Chen Style Taijiquan*, Great Circle Publishing Co, 1998.

Chinese Wushu, Ten *Significant Events in Wushu*. 7, 2003.

Feng Ziqiang in T'ai Chi Magazine [Vol.24, No. 3].

Gaffney, David and Sim, Davidine Siaw-Voon: *Chen Style Taijiquan: The Source of Taiji Boxing*. North Atlantic Books, 2002.

Gu Liuxin and Shen Jiazhen, *Chen Style Taijiquan*. People's Sports Publishing, Beijing (1998).

Henning, Stanley: *General Qi Jiguang's Approach to Martial Arts Training* in Journal of Chen Style Taijiquan Research Association of Hawaii, Vol. 3, No. 2, 1995.

Hong Junsheng: *Practical Boxing Method of Chen Style Taijiquan*, Shandong Science and Technology Press, 1989.

Hucker, Charles O: *China's Imperial Past: An Introduction to Chinese History and Culture*, Stanford University Press, 1975.

Kauz, Herman. *The Aim of Individual Form Practice*, in The Overlook Martial Arts Reader: Classic Writings on Philosophy and Technique. The Overlook press, 1989.

Loehr, James E. *The New Toughness Training for Sports*, Plume, 1995.

Lin Yutang, *The Importance of Living*, William Hienemann Ltd., 1951.

Lin Yutang, *Translations from the Chinese*, Forum Books, 1963.

Ma Hailong, T'ai Chi Magazine, September 2009.

Ma Hong, *Chen Style Taijiquan Method and Theory*. Beijing Sports University Press (1998).

Millinger J. F. and Fang Chaoying: in the *Dictionary of Ming Biography*, edited by L. Carrington Goodrich and Chaoying Fang New York and London: Columbia University Press, 1976.

Ronny Julius C., *Navigating Through Chaos in China*, Mentognost Ltd., 2006.

Schipper, Kristofer. *The Taoist Body*, Pelanduk Publications, 1996.

Schwartz, Benjamin I., *The World of Thought in Ancient China*, Harvard University Press, 1985.

Spence, Jonathan: *The Search For Modern China*, Norton, 1999.

Szymanski, Jarek in Kennedy, Brian and Guo, Elizabeth: *Chinese Martial Arts Training Manuals: A Historical Survey*, North Atlantic Books, 2005.

Unger, Jonathan: *The Class System in Rural China: A Case Study* in *Class and Social Stratification in Post-Revolution China*, edited by Watson, J.L. Cambridge University Press, 1984.

Wang Jie et al. *Chenjiagou Research Paper*, Henan Agricultural University Research Centre, 2006.

Watson, James L., *Class & Social Stratification in Post-Revolution China*, Cambridge University Press, 1984.

Williams, Tom: *Complete Chinese Medicine: A Comprehensive System for Health and Fitness*, Element Books Ltd., 1996.

Xiaolan Zhao. *Traditional Chinese Medicine for Women*, Virago, 2006.

Yu Zhizhou, *Wushu*, Chinese Tourism Press, 2003.

Zhu Tiancai, *Chenjiagou Taijiquan GB interview* in Singapore, 2000.

Zhu Tiancai – An *Examination of Gongfu in Chenjiagou Taijiquan*.

Zhu Tiancai, *Authentic Chenjiagou Taijiquan*. Percetaken Turbo Sdn. Bhd., Malaysia (1994).

About the Authors ...

David Gaffney's interest in East Asian martial arts began in 1980 when he started practicing Wado Ryu Karate training with several noted instructors including Kuniake Sakagami Sensei. Attracted by the holistic nature of the Chinese martial arts, he subsequently trained in the Shaolin Nam Pai Chuan (Southern & Northen Fist) system. During this time he was an active competitor in traditional karate and semi & full contact kickboxing tournaments.

Since 1996 he has focused exclusively on Chen Taijiquan and was formally accepted as a disciple by 19th Generation Chen Taiji Standard Bearer Chen Xiaowang in a traditional Baishi ceremony. In his quest for authentic training, he has travelled to China and the Far East many times to train with some of the leading teachers of Chen Taijiquan.

He has competed successfully in Push Hands competitions at British and International level, winning a gold medal at the 1997 International Atlantic Cup in the Advanced Middleweight division and a silver medal in the 1997

British Open Chinese Martial Arts Championships (-80kgs division) He was awarded an instructor's certificate by the Wenxian Chen Taijiquan Research & Promotion Centre. David was awarded 6th Duan Grade by the Chinese Wushu Association and a Level 3 instructor certificate by the Chen Village Taiji Martial Arts School.

He co-wrote "Chen Style Taijiquan: The Source of Taiji Boxing" with Davidine Siaw-Voon Sim and writes regularly for a number of magazines including T'ai Chi magazine and The Journal of Asian Martial Arts.

Davidine Siaw-Voon Sim has trained with some of the most famous 19th generation Chen Taijiquan teachers including Chen Xiaowang, Chen Xiaoxing, Zhu Tiancai and Chen Zhenglei, among others, making numerous training trips to China and the Far East.

She has competed successfully at British and International level winning a gold medal in the Chen Taijiquan form category at the 1997 International Atlantic Cup, where she was named as "one of the most outstanding performers" by Tai Chi International magazine.

As a writer and recognised authority on Chinese arts and culture, Davidine has been featured on both BBC and Granada TV demonstrating and explaining the benefits of Taijiquan. She co-wrote Chen Style Taijiquan: The Source of Taijiquan with David Gaffney, and has translated many Chinese texts on Chen Style Taijiquan, including Chen Xiaowang's "Chen Family Taijiquan".

Davidine was awarded an instructor's certificate by the Wenxian Chen Taijiquan Research & Promotion Centre. She was awarded 6th Duan Grade by the Chinese Wushu Association and a Level 3 instructor certificate by the Chen Village Taiji Martial Arts School. She teaches in the UK and Europe.

By the same authors...

Chen Style Taijiquan: The Source of Taiji Boxing

What they said...

Journal of Asian Martial Arts: "...soon to be classic book, Chen Style Taijiquan... The publication of Chen Style Taijiquan marks an important landmark in history of the seminal style of taiji."

Stephan Berwick - Taiji Author: "...a landmark book on Chen Taijiquan which raises the bar on martial arts literature in English. Great Job!"

Internal Martial Arts Journal: "This book has been long overdue. This is the first in-depth book on Chen style published in English... All in all, this is a great book for any Taijiquan enthusiasts library, a must for any Chen practitioner as a novice or long time player. I hope it is the first with many more to come in the future. Congratulations to the authors".

Tai Chi Chuan & Internal Arts Magazine: "At last! Here we have a valuable English language resource book on Chen style Taijiquan".

Michael P. Garofalo Taiji Teacher and author: "Very well written and highly informative. Essential reading for all learning the Chen style of Tai Chi".

CHEN STYLE TAIJIQUAN

The Source of Taiji Boxing

Davidine Siaw-Voon Sim
& David Gaffney

Published by North Atlantic Books

ISBN: 1-55643-377-8

"Promoting Traditional Chen Family Taijiquan"

The Essence of Taijiquan was published by Chenjiagou Taijiquan GB

www.chentaijigb.co.uk

Made in the USA
Middletown, DE
29 August 2020